INCREASE
—— IN ——
LEARNING

JOURNAL EDITION

INCREASE
— IN —
LEARNING

Spiritual patterns for obtaining your own answers

JOURNAL EDITION

DAVID A. BEDNAR

DESERET
BOOK

SALT LAKE CITY, UTAH

Visit us at deseretbook.com

First printing in hardbound 2011.
First printing in softbound journal edition 2021.

Library of Congress Cataloging-in-Publication Data
Bednar, David A., author.
  Increase in learning / David A. Bednar.
      p. cm.
  Summary: Focuses upon concepts, patterns, and processes that can help the reader learn for himself or herself the fundamental doctrines and principles of the restored gospel of Jesus Christ.
  Includes bibliographical references and index.
  ISBN 978-1-60908-943-6 (hardbound : alk. paper); ISBN 978-1-62972-911-4 (journal edition)
    1. Learning and scholarship—Religious aspects—Church of Jesus Christ of Latter-day Saints.
2. Prayer—Church of Jesus Christ of Latter-day Saints.   3. Christian life—Mormon authors.
I. Title.
  BX0635.3.B43 2011
  230'.93—dc23   2011037014

Printed in the United States of America
Publishers Printing, Salt Lake City, UT

10   9   8   7   6   5   4   3   2   1

To Susan

Contents

ACKNOWLEDGMENTS

I am grateful to my wife, Susan, for her unwavering love, support, and encouragement. Thanks also to Shauna Swainston for her constant and effective assistance; to Sheri Dew and Jeff Simpson, who patiently and persistently encouraged me to write this book; and to Max Molgard for his helpful feedback. I express my gratitude to the publishing team at Deseret Book: Cory Maxwell, for his careful oversight of the project; Emily Watts, for her insightful editing and expert help in preparing the manuscript for publication; Richard Erickson and Sheryl Dickert Smith for the design; Tonya Facemyer for the typography; Laurel Christensen for her assistance with the accompanying DVD; and Dallas Petersen for handling the online aspects of the project. And I offer my appreciation to an endless list of family members, friends, and Church members and leaders who have taught me and enhanced my gospel learning. To all of these remarkable people, I am both thankful and indebted.

Though I have received assistance from many people, I alone

am responsible for the concepts, ideas, and views expressed in *Increase in Learning*. This book is not an official statement of Church doctrine, policy, or practice.

INCREASE IN LEARNING

I love to learn—and I love learning about learning. This book focuses upon concepts, patterns, and processes that can help you and me learn for ourselves the fundamental doctrines and principles of the restored gospel of Jesus Christ.

The title of this book comes from the ninth chapter of Proverbs: "Give instruction to a wise man, and he will be yet wiser: teach a just man, and he will *increase in learning.* The fear of the Lord is the beginning of wisdom: and the knowledge of the holy is understanding" (Proverbs 9:9–10; emphasis added). This volume discusses why we should and how we can "increase in learning."

Throughout my life I have been drawn to the scriptural injunction to "seek learning, even by study and also by faith" (Doctrine and Covenants 88:118). And I have come to know ever more completely that the true and trustworthy teacher is the Holy Ghost— who shall "teach you all things, and bring all things to your remembrance" (John 14:26) and "teach you the peaceable things of the kingdom" (Doctrine and Covenants 36:2). As a result, I have attempted in this book to link together some of the *spiritual gifts* associated with the companionship of the third member of the Godhead, even the Holy Ghost, and *our individual responsibility to learn* "the doctrine of the kingdom . . . [and] all things . . . that are expedient for you to understand" (Doctrine and Covenants 88:77–78).

I admittedly have had reservations about writing this book, as I have been concerned that words on a page alone cannot fully communicate my intended message or, more important, facilitate the pattern of spiritual learning that is activated by faith in the Lord Jesus Christ. Through the Savior's Atonement, you and I as learners are blessed with the gift of moral agency. Because of that supernal blessing, we are agents with the capacity and power "to act" and are not merely objects "to be acted upon" (2 Nephi 2:26).

Learning and living the gospel of Jesus Christ require us to:

- read and study the scriptures and the teachings of living prophets and apostles—as agents and not as objects;
- pray and ask in faith and submit to the will of the Father—as agents and not as objects; and
- worship and serve God with all of our heart, might, mind, and strength—as agents and not as objects.

I personally do not know of a principle more central, important, or essential to spiritual learning than the principle of acting as agents and not being acted upon as objects.

This volume is not intended to be a quick, casual, or relaxing read. It also does not describe or prescribe specific study habits or methods, and you will not find lengthy lists of recommendations or things "to do." This book does not purport to give definitive doctrinal answers to the pressing questions and issues of our day.

Rather, I invite you throughout the book to engage in various learning experiences so you can increasingly "stand independent"

(Doctrine and Covenants 78:14) and learn how to find answers to your own questions. Consequently, as you progress through the chapters you will need to read, study, ponder, search, ask, knock, record thoughts and feelings, link, connect, revise, rethink, ask again, start again, and, most important, act. For this reason the book is formatted with extra wide margins and blank pages in the back so you can make notes, jot down impressions, and record questions that will facilitate your acting and learning. Experiencing this book will require diligent work and sustained commitment. Only as we "act in doctrine" (Doctrine and Covenants 101:78) can the Holy Ghost ultimately be effective as the teacher of all truth.

As you endeavor to increase in learning, please remember that the doctrines and principles of the restored gospel should be considered in their totality. In other words, attempting to understand a doctrine or principle by examining a single scripture or prophetic statement in isolation from all else that has been revealed on the subject is generally misguided. True doctrines and principles are emphasized repeatedly in the standard works, by the prophets and apostles, and through the illuminating and confirming power of the Holy Ghost.

In addition to the text material contained in this volume, other learning resources are available online at desbook.com/learning. The video segments available there comprise an interview in which Sister Bednar and I discuss the concepts in the book as well as a live Q&A discussion conducted with a group of young adults. Throughout the book, the icon ▶ in the margin marks relevant segments of the video presentation. Please remember, however, that the written text, the questions to consider, the questions you pose at the end of each chapter, the readings, and the additional resources are not complete in and of themselves. Each has been designed to complement and enhance the others.

At the end of each chapter are related readings that expand on and emphasize many of the concepts taught. Most of these readings are taken from talks that were reprinted in the *Ensign*. In some cases, the wording has been altered slightly in this book to eliminate occasion-specific references and repetition.

My hope is that the combination of your faith in Heavenly Father and the Savior, your willingness to act as an agent, the text, and the learning experiences in which you will engage will invite the Holy Ghost to help you more fully understand basic gospel truths and a powerful spiritual pattern—to the end that each of us may *INCREASE IN LEARNING*.

CHAPTER ONE

An Individual
Responsibility to Learn

Each and every member of The Church of Jesus Christ of Latter-day Saints bears a *personal* responsibility to learn and live the truths of the Savior's restored gospel and to receive by proper authority the ordinances of salvation. We should not expect the Church as an organization to teach or tell us all of the things we need to know and do to become devoted disciples and endure valiantly to the end (see Doctrine and Covenants 121:29). Rather, our individual responsibility is to learn what we should learn, to live as we know we should live, and to become what the Master would have us become.

As young Joseph Smith returned to his home from the Sacred Grove immediately after the appearance of the Father and the Son, he spoke first with his mother. As he "leaned up to the fireplace, [his] mother inquired what the matter was. [Joseph] replied, 'Never mind, all is well—I am well enough off.' [He] then said to [his] mother, '*I have learned for myself* . . . '" (Joseph Smith—History 1:20; emphasis added).

The overarching purpose of Heavenly Father's great plan of happiness is to provide His spirit children with opportunities to

1

learn. The moral agency afforded to all of Father's children through the plan of salvation and the Atonement of Jesus Christ is divinely designed to facilitate our learning. As Elder Bruce C. Hafen has explained, because of "the Atonement of Jesus Christ [we may] *learn* from our experience without being *condemned* by that experience" ("Eve Heard All These Things," 32; emphasis added).

The Savior said, "Learn of me, and listen to my words; walk in the meekness of my Spirit, and you shall have peace in me" (Doctrine and Covenants 19:23). We are assisted in learning of and listening to the words of Christ by the Holy Ghost, even the third member of the Godhead. The Holy Ghost reveals and witnesses the truth of all things and brings all things to our remembrance (see John 14:26; 16:13; Moroni 10:5; Doctrine and Covenants 39:6). The Holy Ghost is the teacher who kindles within us an abiding love of and for learning.

See video segment 3

We repeatedly are admonished in the revelations to ask in faith when we lack knowledge (see James 1:5–6), to "seek learning, even by study and also by faith" (Doctrine and Covenants 88:118), and to inquire of God that we might receive instruction from His Spirit (see Doctrine and Covenants 6:14) and know "mysteries which are great and marvelous" (Doctrine and Covenants 6:11). The restored Church of Jesus Christ exists today to "[preserve] in safety" (Doctrine and Covenants 42:56) the holy scriptures, the pure doctrine, and the saving ordinances of the Savior's gospel—and to help individuals and families learn about and receive these supernal blessings.

THE IMPORTANCE OF LEARNING IN THE LATTER DAYS

Our individual responsibility to learn truth, to love truth, and to live according to truth is increasingly important in a world that is "in commotion" (Doctrine and Covenants 45:26) and grows ever more confused and wicked. We cannot expect simply to attend Church meetings and to participate in programs and thereby receive all of the spiritual fortification and protection that will enable us to "withstand in the evil day, and having done all, to stand" (Ephesians 6:13). Certainly inspired leaders and activities help and support individual and family efforts to grow spiritually. But the ultimate responsibility for developing spiritual strength and stamina rests upon each and every member of the Church.

In the grand division of all of God's creations, there are things to act and things to be acted upon (see 2 Nephi 2:13–14). As sons and daughters of our Heavenly Father, we have been blessed with the gift of agency, the capacity and power of independent action. Endowed with agency we are agents, and we primarily are to act and not simply be acted upon—especially as we seek to obtain and apply spiritual knowledge.

Learning by faith and learning from experience are two of the central features of the Father's plan of happiness. The Savior preserved moral agency through the Atonement and made it possible for us to act and to learn. Lucifer's rebellion against the plan sought to destroy the agency of man, and his intent was that we as learners would only be acted upon.

Consider the question posed by Heavenly Father to Adam in the Garden of Eden, "Where art thou?" (Genesis 3:9). Obviously the Father knew where Adam was hiding, but He nonetheless asked the question. Why? A wise and loving Father enabled His child to act in the learning process and not merely be acted upon. There was no one-way lecture to a disobedient child, as perhaps many of us might be inclined to deliver. Rather, the Father helped Adam as a learner to act as an agent and appropriately exercise his agency.

See video segment 11

Recall how Nephi desired to know about the things his father, Lehi, had seen in the vision of the tree of life. Interestingly, the Spirit of the Lord began the tutorial with Nephi by asking the following question, "Behold, what desirest thou?" (1 Nephi 11:2). Clearly the Spirit knew what Nephi desired. So why ask the question? The Holy Ghost was helping Nephi to act in the learning process and not simply be acted upon.

See video segment 1

From these examples we recognize that as learners, you and I are to act and be "doers of the word" (James 1:22) and not simply hearers who are only acted upon. Are you and I truly agents who act and seek to learn, or are we waiting to be acted upon and relying exclusively on other people to teach us? To become and remain spiritually firm, steadfast, and immovable in the world that does now and will yet exist, we should exercise our moral agency in accordance with true principles and seek learning by patiently and persistently asking, seeking, and knocking (see 3 Nephi 14:7).

Examples of Latter-day Learners

True disciples of the Lord Jesus Christ love truth and are "anxiously engaged" (Doctrine and Covenants 58:27) as learners.

"For he shall lay his hands upon thee, and thou shalt receive the Holy Ghost, and thy time shall be given to writing, and to *learning much*" (Doctrine and Covenants 25:8; emphasis added).

"Hearken, O ye people of my church; for verily I say unto you that these things were spoken unto you for your profit and *learning*" (Doctrine and Covenants 46:1; emphasis added).

"Verily I say unto you my friends, I speak unto you with my voice, even the voice of my Spirit, that I may show unto you my will concerning your brethren in the land of Zion, many of whom are truly humble and are seeking diligently to *learn* wisdom and to find truth" (Doctrine and Covenants 97:1; emphasis added).

The powerful examples of the following Latter-day learners highlight the importance of continuously seeking learning by study and also by faith (see Doctrine and Covenants 88:118).

Joseph Smith

The Prophet Joseph Smith was the greatest learner in the dispensation of the fulness of times. He was a sincere and eager student, his teachers were members of the Godhead and angels, and his curriculum was focused upon the truths of eternity. Joseph is the quintessential example of a humble and diligent learner.

Joseph "loved learning," observed George Q. Cannon. "He loved knowledge for its righteous power. Through the tribulations which had surrounded him from the day when first he made known to a skeptical world his communion with the heavens, he had been ever advancing in the acquisition of intelligence. The Lord had commanded him to study, and he was obeying. . . . His mind, quickened by the Holy Spirit, grasped with readiness all true principles, and one by one he mastered these branches and became in them a teacher" (*Life of Joseph Smith,* 199).

The majesty, the scope, and the ongoing impact of Joseph Smith's mortal ministry certainly were not the result of worldly education and privileged position. Joseph's lack of formal schooling is a well-established fact. Because he was a farm boy from a poor family, he did not attend school as frequently as did other children. His formal education was limited to a study of the rudiments of reading, writing, and arithmetic (see Joseph Smith, "History of the Life of Joseph Smith" [1832], n. p.) Joseph described himself as "an obscure boy, only between fourteen and fifteen years of age, and my circumstances in life such as to make a boy of no consequence in the world . . . who was doomed to the necessity of obtaining a scanty maintenance by his daily labor" (Joseph Smith—History 1:22–23).

Emma Hale Smith provided notable commentary about her husband's limited education. "Joseph Smith could neither write nor dictate a coherent and well-worded letter, let alone dictating a book like the Book of Mormon. And, though I was an active participant in the scenes that transpired, and was present during the translation of the plates, and had cognizance of things as they transpired, it is marvelous to me, 'a marvel and a wonder,' as much so as to any one else" (in Joseph Smith III, "Last Testimony of Sister Emma," 289–90).

During the work of translation Emma acted temporarily as a scribe. She reported: "'[Joseph] could not pronounce the word Sariah.' And one time while translating, where [the text] speaks of the walls of Jerusalem, he stopped and said, 'Emma, did Jerusalem have walls surrounding it?' When [Emma] informed him it had, he replied, 'O, I thought I was deceived'" (in E. C. Briggs, "Brother Joseph Smith," 396).

Though he had meager access to opportunities for academic advancement, Joseph's heavenly tutorials and experiences produced in him an insatiable desire to learn that was evident throughout his life. And he diligently taught the Saints likewise to seek learning and the knowledge that comes from God.

"The things of God are of deep import; and time, and experience, and careful and ponderous and solemn thoughts can only find them out. Thy mind, O man! if thou wilt lead a soul unto salvation, must stretch as high as the utmost heavens, and search into and contemplate the darkest abyss, and the broad expanse of eternity—thou must commune with God. How much more dignified and noble are the thoughts of God, than the vain imaginations of the human heart! . . .

" . . . Let honesty, and sobriety, and candor, and solemnity, and virtue, and pureness, and meekness, and simplicity crown our heads in every place; and in fine, become as little children, without malice, guile or hypocrisy. And now, brethren, after your tribulations, if you do these things, and exercise fervent prayer and faith in the sight of God always, He shall give unto you knowledge by His Holy Spirit, yea by the unspeakable gift of the Holy Ghost" (*Teachings: Joseph Smith,* 267–68).

George A. Smith, while serving in the First Presidency, stated: "Joseph Smith taught that every man and woman should seek the Lord for wisdom, that they might get knowledge from Him who is the fountain of knowledge; and the promises of the gospel, as revealed, were such as to authorize us to believe, that by taking this course we should gain the object of our pursuit" (*Teachings: Joseph Smith,* 266).

"When you climb up a ladder, you must begin at the bottom, and ascend step by step, until you arrive at the top; and so it is with the principles of the gospel—you must begin with the first, and go on until you learn all the principles of exaltation. But it will be a great while after you have passed through the veil before you will have learned them. It is not all to be comprehended in this world; it will be a great work to learn our salvation and exaltation even beyond the grave" (*Teachings: Joseph Smith,* 268).

Joseph Smith and his counselors in the First Presidency gave the following instructions to the Saints who were gathering to

Nauvoo: "To those who . . . can assist in this great work, we say, let them come to this place; by so doing they will not only assist in the rolling on of the Kingdom, but be in a situation where they can have the advantages of instruction from the Presidency and other authorities of the Church, and rise higher and higher in the scale of intelligence until they can 'comprehend with all saints what is the breadth and length, and depth and height; and to know the love of Christ, which passeth knowledge' [Ephesians 3:18–19].

"God hath not revealed anything to Joseph, but what He will make known unto the Twelve, and even the least Saint may know all things as fast as he is able to bear them, for the day must come when no man need say to his neighbor, Know ye the Lord; for all shall know Him . . . from the least to the greatest" (*Teachings: Joseph Smith*, 268).

Each of us can be blessed abundantly as we come to understand our individual responsibility to learn as well as what we should learn, how we can learn, and ultimately what we are to become by following the example of the greatest of all latter-day learners, even the Prophet of the Restoration, Joseph Smith.

Brigham Young

Although President Brigham Young had only eleven days of formal schooling, he understood the need for learning both the wisdom of God and the things of the world. He was a furniture maker, a missionary, a colonizer, a governor, and the Lord's prophet.

I marvel at both the way Brigham Young learned and how much he learned. He never ceased learning from the revelations of the Lord, from the scriptures, and from good books. Perhaps President Young was such a consummate learner precisely because he was not constrained unduly by the arbitrary boundaries so often imposed through the structures and processes of formal education. He clearly learned to love learning. He clearly learned how to learn. He ultimately became a powerful disciple and teacher precisely because he first was an effective learner.

President Brigham Young repeatedly taught that the object of our mortal existence is to learn (see *Discourses of Brigham Young,* 87). The following statements by President Young emphasize this truth.

"The religion embraced by the Latter-day Saints, if only slightly understood, prompts them to search diligently after knowledge. There is no other people in existence more eager to see, hear, learn, and understand truth" (*Teachings: Brigham Young,* 194).

"Put forth your ability to learn as fast as you can, and gather all the strength of mind and principle of faith you possibly can, and then distribute your knowledge to the people" (*Teachings: Brigham Young,* 194).

"This work is a progressive work, this doctrine that is taught the Latter-day Saints in its nature is exalting, increasing, expanding and extending broader and broader until we can know as we are known, see as we are seen" (*Teachings: Brigham Young,* 87).

"We are in the school [of mortality] and keep learning, and we do not expect to cease learning while we live on earth; and when we pass through the veil, we expect still to continue to learn and increase our fund of information. That may appear a strange idea to some; but it is for the plain and simple reason that we are not capacitated to receive all knowledge at once. We must therefore receive a little here and a little there" (*Teachings: Brigham Young,* 87).

"We might ask, when shall we cease to learn? I will give you my opinion about it: never, never" (*Teachings: Brigham Young,* 195).

Brigham Young's acceptance of and conversion to the gospel of Jesus Christ fueled his unceasing curiosity and love of learning, and he testified that we are never left alone or on our own.

"My knowledge is, if you will follow the teachings of Jesus Christ and his Apostles, as recorded in the New Testament, every man and woman will be put in possession of the Holy Ghost. . . . They will know things that are, that will be, and that have been. They will understand things in heaven, things on the earth, and things under the earth, things of time, and things of eternity, according to their several callings and capacities" (*Teachings: Brigham Young,* 68).

The ongoing spiritual and personal learning evidenced in the life of Brigham Young is a worthy example for you and for me.

Gordon B. Hinckley

Gordon B. Hinckley was a lifelong learner. As a boy he lived with his family "in a large old house. One room was called the library. It had a solid table and a good lamp, three or four comfortable chairs with good light, and books in cases that lined the walls. There were many volumes—the acquisitions of [his] father and mother over a period of many years.

"We were never forced to read them, but they were placed where they were handy and where we could get at them whenever we wished.

"There was quiet in that room. It was understood that it was a place to study.

" . . . there was an environment . . . of learning. I would not have you believe that we were great scholars. But we were exposed to great literature, great ideas from great thinkers, and the language of men and women who thought deeply and wrote beautifully" (*Teachings of Gordon B. Hinckley*, 170).

Gordon B. Hinckley completed high school in 1928 and enrolled at the University of Utah that fall. As he progressed in his undergraduate studies, he planned on pursuing a graduate degree in journalism. He finished his university studies in 1932 and then served in the European Mission from 1933 to 1935. Upon returning home from his mission, he set aside his ambition to obtain a graduate degree in order to accept employment as the executive secretary of the Church Radio, Publicity, and Mission Literature Committee. Except for a brief period in the 1940s, he spent the remainder of his life working and serving at Church headquarters in Salt Lake City.

All who knew and worked with Gordon B. Hinckley marveled at his constant curiosity and desire to learn. The curriculum of his life exposed him to the processes of managing people and organizations, the complexities of the financial world, the exactness of architecture and construction, the intricacies of educational institutions and procedures, and a multitude of other topics and skills. His knowledge and mastery of these various disciplines was inspiring. Gordon B. Hinckley always was learning.

As President of the Church, he taught frequently and powerfully about our ongoing responsibility to learn.

"None of us . . . knows enough. The learning process is an endless process. We must read, we must observe, we must assimilate, and we must ponder that to which we expose our minds. . . .

" . . . You cannot afford to stop. You must not rest in your development. . . . There is so much to learn and so little time in which to learn it" (*Teachings of Gordon B. Hinckley*, 298–99).

"There is . . . incumbent upon you, you who are members of The Church of Jesus Christ of Latter-day Saints, the responsibility to observe the commandment to continue to study and to learn. Said the Lord: 'Seek ye out of the best books words of wisdom; seek learning, even by study and also by faith' (Doctrine and Covenants 88:118).

" . . . Our search for truth must be broad, . . . we are to learn 'of things both in heaven and in the earth, and under the earth; things which have been, things which are, things which must shortly come to pass; things which are at home, things which are abroad; the wars and the perplexities of the nations, and the judgments which are on the land; and a knowledge also of countries and of kingdoms' (Doctrine and Covenants 88:79).

"What a charge has been laid upon us to grow constantly toward eternity. . . . [Ours] must be a ceaseless quest for truth" (*Teachings of Gordon B. Hinckley,* 300).

"None of us can assume that he has learned enough. As the door closes on one phase of life, it opens on another, where we must continue to pursue knowledge. Ours ought to be a ceaseless quest for truth" (*Teachings of Gordon B. Hinckley,* 301).

"When all is said and done, we are all students. If the day ever comes when we quit learning, look out. We will just atrophy and die. We all can learn and learn well" (*Teachings of Gordon B. Hinckley,* 302).

"We must go on growing. We must continuously learn. It is a divinely given mandate that we go on adding to our knowledge" (*Teachings of Gordon B. Hinckley,* 303).

"With all of our learning, let us also learn of him. With all of our study, we need to seek knowledge of the Master. That knowledge will complement in a wonderful way our secular train-ing and will give us character and a fulness to life that can come in no other way" ("With All Thy Getting Get Understanding," 5).

Certainly each of us can learn and benefit from the example of continuous learning that was demonstrated in the life of President Gordon B. Hinckley.

The extraordinary accomplishments and prominence of Presidents Joseph Smith, Brigham Young, and Gordon B. Hinckley may cause us to compare our puny progress to theirs and conclude that we cannot learn as they learned or become what they became. Such a conclusion would be ill founded and false. Position and public notoriety are not the issues that matter to the Lord. The patterns of learning we can identify in the lives of these great latter-day prophets are applicable to all of us—strong desire and yearning for increased knowledge, intense spiritual and intellectual curiosity and seeking, diligent and persistent work, and the absolute neces-sity for the companionship and influence of the Holy Ghost. These same crucial characteristics likewise are evident in the following examples of ordinary members of the Church—over time and from around the world.

Eduardo Contreras

Eduardo Contreras, one of five children reared by a widowed mother in Cordoba, Argentina, left school at the age of eight to find work so he could help support his family. He worked at vari-ous jobs, including shining shoes, making bricks, picking potatoes, and selling newspapers, until as a young man he had a chance to be employed full-time with the municipal government.

Eduardo later married, and he and his wife, Maria, had five children of their own, but he never had the opportunity for additional education by the time those children began to leave home. It did not seem likely that he would ever achieve his desire to learn to read.

Then, in front of his home one day, Eduardo chased away several local boys who were heckling two missionaries from The Church of Jesus Christ of Latter-day Saints. He talked with and listened to the missionaries and soon began taking the discussions with his wife.

"I had a hard time understanding anything they said because they spoke little Spanish," Eduardo relates, "but they showed me a pamphlet that had pictures of the Savior and of Joseph Smith in the Sacred Grove. I thought the pictures they showed us and the things that they taught us were beautiful." Eduardo and Maria, along with their youngest son, Osvaldo, were baptized.

After his baptism, Eduardo felt a strong desire to read the Book of Mormon the missionaries had given to him. "How do I learn to read?" he asked his wife. Maria told him to look at the letters, try to sound them out, and then speak out loud.

With a prayer in his heart, Eduardo sat down to study in a shady spot in the backyard of his home. Maria reports that she never would have imagined what happened next. Through the kitchen window, she heard Eduardo slowly sounding out letters and words. "Suddenly I heard him speaking rapidly. I realized that he was reading—fluently. Less than half an hour had passed, and he was reading!"

In the yard, Eduardo was so immersed in his study that he had not realized he was reading. But as he read, he recalls, "I felt a fire burning within me." Surprised, Eduardo called to his wife, "Mami, what is happening to me?"

Maria responded, "It's the Spirit of the Lord. You are reading fluently."

"The day I learned to read is also the day I gained my testimony of the Book of Mormon and its power," declared Eduardo. He started getting up at 4:00 A.M. to read the Book of Mormon and other scriptures before going to work. And with help from a dedicated ward member, he also learned to write.

Today Brother Contreras enjoys all the blessings of literacy. He says, "For me the Book of Mormon was the door," the entrance into a life changed by the gospel of Jesus Christ and a desire to learn fueled by the Holy Ghost. "The Book of Mormon was everything to me. It *is* everything to me. I feel the Spirit every time I open it to read" (see Morris, "A Fire Burning Within Me," 66–67).

Edna Amburo

When Edna Amburo was introduced to The Church of Jesus Christ of Latter-day Saints in Papua New Guinea, she had difficulty reading the Book of Mormon. Not only was it hard for her to understand the book, but her friends declared she was "going to the fire" for reading it. "All my friends told me to burn the book," she said, "but I decided not to burn it because I felt the Book of Mormon was the word of God."

Receiving a witness of the truthfulness of the restored gospel by the Spirit of the Lord, Edna was baptized in 1990. Shortly thereafter, she was called to teach the Book of Mormon to seminary students.

Edna wondered, "How am I going to teach? I am not an educated woman. I am not a good speaker in English, and I am not a good writer. I left school in grade five."

Fasting and praying, Edna turned to the Lord for help to understand the Book of Mormon and to become an effective teacher. As she acted in faith and read the Book of Mormon, Edna accepted the invitation in Moroni 10 to "ask God, the Eternal

Father, in the name of Christ, if these things are not true" (v. 4). Edna said of her experience, "I saw it was true. I got peace in my heart. I got joy. And I was happy that I was going to teach seminary. I really love the Book of Mormon. I understand it now."

Sister Amburo has grown both spiritually and intellectually with help from Heavenly Father. "Step by step, I came along. The Church has helped me a lot. It is a learning church. I am thankful my Heavenly Father brought me into this church, and I am thankful for the Prophet Joseph Smith, who restored it to the earth. I love it with all my heart. I am very happy" (see Morris, "'One Talk' in Papua New Guinea," 28).

SUMMARY

See video segment 12

You and I are here upon the earth to prepare for eternity, to learn how to learn, to learn things that are temporally important and eternally essential, and to assist others in learning wisdom and truth (see Doctrine and Covenants 97:1). Understanding who we are, where we came from, and why we are upon the earth places upon each of us a great responsibility both to learn how to learn and to learn to love learning.

Spiritual knowledge cannot be given by or borrowed from another person. Shortcuts to the desired destination do not exist. Cramming for the ultimate final examination on the day of judgment is not an option. In this eternally important endeavor, the Lord's pattern is "line upon line, precept upon precept, here a little and there a little; and blessed are those who hearken unto my precepts, and lend an ear unto my counsel, for they shall *learn* wisdom; for unto him that receiveth I will give more" (2 Nephi 28:30; emphasis added). The efficacy of the law of the harvest clearly applies to our individual responsibility to learn and live gospel truths: "For whatsoever a man soweth, that shall he also reap" (Galatians 6:7).

QUESTIONS TO CONSIDER

1. As a learner, what are the implications for me of knowing that I am an *agent* blessed with agency who can act rather than an *object* that is merely acted upon?

2. How will understanding and effectively fulfilling my *individual responsibility* as a learner prepare me for the world in which I do now and will yet live?

3. What am I *learning about learning* from the examples of latter-day learners described in this chapter?

YOUR OWN QUESTIONS TO CONSIDER

1. _____

2. _____

3. _____

The video segments related to this chapter can be found at

desbook.com/learning

Related Readings
for Chapter One

An increased yearning to learn is one of the important spiritual effects that grows out of putting off "the natural man and [becoming] a saint through the atonement of Christ the Lord" (Mosiah 3:19). Importantly, however, the process of putting off the natural man is initiated by "[yielding] to the enticings of the Holy Spirit." The Spirit of the Lord is the only true and trustworthy teacher who can "teach [us] all things, and bring all things to [our] remembrance" (John 14:26), "teach [us] the peaceable things of the kingdom" (Doctrine and Covenants 36:2), and kindle within us an abiding love of and for learning.

The following readings all focus upon the role of the Holy Ghost in fulfilling our personal responsibility to learn and live the truths of the Savior's restored gospel and to receive by proper authority the ordinances of salvation. The readings also highlight some of the spiritual gifts and blessings associated with the constant companionship of the third member of the Godhead.

1 Nephi, Chapters 11 through 14

Read and study 1 Nephi 11–14. Pay particular attention to how the Spirit both asks questions and encourages Nephi to "look" as active elements in the learning process.

1 Nephi 11

1. For it came to pass after I had desired to know the things that my father had seen, and believing that the Lord was able to make them known unto me, as I sat pondering in mine heart I was caught away in the Spirit of the Lord, yea, into an exceedingly high mountain, which I never had before seen, and upon which I never had before set my foot.

2. And the Spirit said unto me: Behold, what desirest thou?

3. And I said: I desire to behold the things which my father saw.

4. And the Spirit said unto me: Believest thou that thy father saw the tree of which he hath spoken?

5. And I said: Yea, thou knowest that I believe all the words of my father.

6. And when I had spoken these words, the Spirit cried with a loud voice, saying: Hosanna to the Lord, the most high God; for he is God over all the earth, yea, even above all. And blessed art thou, Nephi, because thou believest in the Son of the most high God; wherefore, thou shalt behold the things which thou hast desired.

7. And behold this thing shall be given unto thee for a sign, that after thou hast beheld the tree which bore the fruit which thy father tasted, thou shalt also behold a man descending out of heaven, and him shall ye witness; and after ye have witnessed him ye shall bear record that it is the Son of God.

8. And it came to pass that the Spirit said unto me: Look! And I looked and beheld a tree; and it was like unto the tree which my father had seen; and the beauty thereof was far beyond, yea, exceeding of all beauty; and the whiteness thereof did exceed the whiteness of the driven snow.

9. And it came to pass after I had seen the tree, I said unto the Spirit: I behold thou hast shown unto me the tree which is precious above all.

10. And he said unto me: What desirest thou?

11. And I said unto him: To know the interpretation thereof—for I spake unto him as a man speaketh; for I beheld that he was in the form of a man; yet nevertheless, I knew that it was the Spirit of the Lord; and he spake unto me as a man speaketh with another.

12. And it came to pass that he said unto me: Look! And I looked as if to look upon him, and I saw him not; for he had gone from before my presence.

13. And it came to pass that I looked and beheld the great city of Jerusalem, and also other cities. And I beheld the city of Nazareth; and in the city of Nazareth I beheld a virgin, and she was exceedingly fair and white.

14. And it came to pass that I saw the heavens open; and an angel came down and stood before me; and he said unto me: Nephi, what beholdest thou?

15. And I said unto him: A virgin, most beautiful and fair above all other virgins.

16. And he said unto me: Knowest thou the condescension of God?

17. And I said unto him: I know that he loveth his children; nevertheless, I do not know the meaning of all things.

18. And he said unto me: Behold, the virgin whom thou seest is the mother of the Son of God, after the manner of the flesh.

19. And it came to pass that I beheld that she was carried away in the Spirit; and after she had been carried away in the Spirit for the space of a time the angel spake unto me, saying: Look!

20. And I looked and beheld the virgin again, bearing a child in her arms.

21. And the angel said unto me: Behold the Lamb of God, yea, even the Son of the Eternal Father! Knowest thou the meaning of the tree which thy father saw?

22. And I answered him, saying: Yea, it is the love of God, which sheddeth itself abroad in the hearts of the children of men; wherefore, it is the most desirable above all things.

23. And he spake unto me, saying: Yea, and the most joyous to the soul.

24. And after he had said these words, he said unto me: Look! And I looked, and I beheld the Son of God going forth among the children of men; and I saw many fall down at his feet and worship him.

25. And it came to pass that I beheld that the rod of iron, which my father had seen, was the word of God, which led to the fountain of living waters, or to the tree of life; which waters are a representation of the love of God; and I also beheld that the tree of life was a representation of the love of God.

26. And the angel said unto me again: Look and behold the condescension of God!

27. And I looked and beheld the Redeemer of the world, of

whom my father had spoken; and I also beheld the prophet who should prepare the way before him. And the Lamb of God went forth and was baptized of him; and after he was baptized, I beheld the heavens open, and the Holy Ghost come down out of heaven and abide upon him in the form of a dove.

28. And I beheld that he went forth ministering unto the people, in power and great glory; and the multitudes were gathered together to hear him; and I beheld that they cast him out from among them.

29. And I also beheld twelve others following him. And it came to pass that they were carried away in the Spirit from before my face, and I saw them not.

30. And it came to pass that the angel spake unto me again, saying: Look! And I looked, and I beheld the heavens open again, and I saw angels descending upon the children of men; and they did minister unto them.

31. And he spake unto me again, saying: Look! And I looked, and I beheld the Lamb of God going forth among the children of men. And I beheld multitudes of people who were sick, and who were afflicted with all manner of diseases, and with devils and unclean spirits; and the angel spake and showed all these things unto me. And they were healed by the power of the Lamb of God; and the devils and the unclean spirits were cast out.

32. And it came to pass that the angel spake unto me again, saying: Look! And I looked and beheld the Lamb of God, that he was taken by the people; yea, the Son of the everlasting God was judged of the world; and I saw and bear record.

33. And I, Nephi, saw that he was lifted up upon the cross and slain for the sins of the world.

34. And after he was slain I saw the multitudes of the earth,

that they were gathered together to fight against the apostles of the Lamb; for thus were the twelve called by the angel of the Lord.

35. And the multitude of the earth was gathered together; and I beheld that they were in a large and spacious building, like unto the building which my father saw. And the angel of the Lord spake unto me again, saying: Behold the world and the wisdom thereof; yea, behold the house of Israel hath gathered together to fight against the twelve apostles of the Lamb.

36. And it came to pass that I saw and bear record, that the great and spacious building was the pride of the world; and it fell, and the fall thereof was exceedingly great. And the angel of the Lord spake unto me again, saying: Thus shall be the destruction of all nations, kindreds, tongues, and people, that shall fight against the twelve apostles of the Lamb.

1 Nephi 12

1. And it came to pass that the angel said unto me: Look, and behold thy seed, and also the seed of thy brethren. And I looked and beheld the land of promise; and I beheld multitudes of people, yea, even as it were in number as many as the sand of the sea.

2. And it came to pass that I beheld multitudes gathered together to battle, one against the other; and I beheld wars, and rumors of wars, and great slaughters with the sword among my people.

3. And it came to pass that I beheld many generations pass away, after the manner of wars and contentions in the land; and I beheld many cities, yea, even that I did not number them.

4. And it came to pass that I saw a mist of darkness on the face of the land of promise; and I saw lightnings, and I heard thunderings, and earthquakes, and all manner of tumultuous noises; and

I saw the earth and the rocks, that they rent; and I saw mountains tumbling into pieces; and I saw the plains of the earth, that they were broken up; and I saw many cities that they were sunk; and I saw many that they were burned with fire; and I saw many that did tumble to the earth, because of the quaking thereof.

5. And it came to pass after I saw these things, I saw the vapor of darkness, that it passed from off the face of the earth; and behold, I saw multitudes who had not fallen because of the great and terrible judgments of the Lord.

6. And I saw the heavens open, and the Lamb of God descending out of heaven; and he came down and showed himself unto them.

7. And I also saw and bear record that the Holy Ghost fell upon twelve others; and they were ordained of God, and chosen.

8. And the angel spake unto me, saying: Behold the twelve disciples of the Lamb, who are chosen to minister unto thy seed.

9. And he said unto me: Thou rememberest the twelve apostles of the Lamb? Behold they are they who shall judge the twelve tribes of Israel; wherefore, the twelve ministers of thy seed shall be judged of them; for ye are of the house of Israel.

10. And these twelve ministers whom thou beholdest shall judge thy seed. And, behold, they are righteous forever; for because of their faith in the Lamb of God their garments are made white in his blood.

11. And the angel said unto me: Look! And I looked, and beheld three generations pass away in righteousness; and their garments were white even like unto the Lamb of God. And the angel said unto me: These are made white in the blood of the Lamb, because of their faith in him.

12. And I, Nephi, also saw many of the fourth generation who passed away in righteousness.

13. And it came to pass that I saw the multitudes of the earth gathered together.

14. And the angel said unto me: Behold thy seed, and also the seed of thy brethren.

15. And it came to pass that I looked and beheld the people of my seed gathered together in multitudes against the seed of my brethren; and they were gathered together to battle.

16. And the angel spake unto me, saying: Behold the fountain of filthy water which thy father saw; yea, even the river of which he spake; and the depths thereof are the depths of hell.

17. And the mists of darkness are the temptations of the devil, which blindeth the eyes, and hardeneth the hearts of the children of men, and leadeth them away into broad roads, that they perish and are lost.

18. And the large and spacious building, which thy father saw, is vain imaginations and the pride of the children of men. And a great and a terrible gulf divideth them; yea, even the word of the justice of the Eternal God, and the Messiah who is the Lamb of God, of whom the Holy Ghost beareth record, from the beginning of the world until this time, and from this time henceforth and forever.

19. And while the angel spake these words, I beheld and saw that the seed of my brethren did contend against my seed, according to the word of the angel; and because of the pride of my seed, and the temptations of the devil, I beheld that the seed of my brethren did overpower the people of my seed.

20. And it came to pass that I beheld, and saw the people of the seed of my brethren that they had overcome my seed; and they went forth in multitudes upon the face of the land.

21. And I saw them gathered together in multitudes; and I saw

wars and rumors of wars among them; and in wars and rumors of wars I saw many generations pass away.

22. And the angel said unto me: Behold these shall dwindle in unbelief.

23. And it came to pass that I beheld, after they had dwindled in unbelief they became a dark, and loathsome, and a filthy people, full of idleness and all manner of abominations.

1 Nephi 13

1. And it came to pass that the angel spake unto me, saying: Look! And I looked and beheld many nations and kingdoms.

2. And the angel said unto me: What beholdest thou? And I said: I behold many nations and kingdoms.

3. And he said unto me: These are the nations and kingdoms of the Gentiles.

4. And it came to pass that I saw among the nations of the Gentiles the formation of a great church.

5. And the angel said unto me: Behold the formation of a church which is most abominable above all other churches, which slayeth the saints of God, yea, and tortureth them and bindeth them down, and yoketh them with a yoke of iron, and bringeth them down into captivity.

6. And it came to pass that I beheld this great and abominable church; and I saw the devil that he was the founder of it.

7. And I also saw gold, and silver, and silks, and scarlets, and fine-twined linen, and all manner of precious clothing; and I saw many harlots.

8. And the angel spake unto me, saying: Behold the gold, and the silver, and the silks, and the scarlets, and the fine-twined linen,

and the precious clothing, and the harlots, are the desires of this great and abominable church.

9. And also for the praise of the world do they destroy the saints of God, and bring them down into captivity.

10. And it came to pass that I looked and beheld many waters; and they divided the Gentiles from the seed of my brethren.

11. And it came to pass that the angel said unto me: Behold the wrath of God is upon the seed of thy brethren.

12. And I looked and beheld a man among the Gentiles, who was separated from the seed of my brethren by the many waters; and I beheld the Spirit of God, that it came down and wrought upon the man; and he went forth upon the many waters, even unto the seed of my brethren, who were in the promised land.

13. And it came to pass that I beheld the Spirit of God, that it wrought upon other Gentiles; and they went forth out of captivity, upon the many waters.

14. And it came to pass that I beheld many multitudes of the Gentiles upon the land of promise; and I beheld the wrath of God, that it was upon the seed of my brethren; and they were scattered before the Gentiles and were smitten.

15. And I beheld the Spirit of the Lord, that it was upon the Gentiles, and they did prosper and obtain the land for their inheritance; and I beheld that they were white, and exceedingly fair and beautiful, like unto my people before they were slain.

16. And it came to pass that I, Nephi, beheld that the Gentiles who had gone forth out of captivity did humble themselves before the Lord; and the power of the Lord was with them.

17. And I beheld that their mother Gentiles were gathered together upon the waters, and upon the land also, to battle against them.

18. And I beheld that the power of God was with them, and

also that the wrath of God was upon all those that were gathered together against them to battle.

19. And I, Nephi, beheld that the Gentiles that had gone out of captivity were delivered by the power of God out of the hands of all other nations.

20. And it came to pass that I, Nephi, beheld that they did prosper in the land; and I beheld a book, and it was carried forth among them.

21. And the angel said unto me: Knowest thou the meaning of the book?

22. And I said unto him: I know not.

23. And he said: Behold it proceedeth out of the mouth of a Jew. And I, Nephi, beheld it; and he said unto me: The book that thou beholdest is a record of the Jews, which contains the covenants of the Lord, which he hath made unto the house of Israel; and it also containeth many of the prophecies of the holy prophets; and it is a record like unto the engravings which are upon the plates of brass, save there are not so many; nevertheless, they contain the covenants of the Lord, which he hath made unto the house of Israel; wherefore, they are of great worth unto the Gentiles.

24. And the angel of the Lord said unto me: Thou hast beheld that the book proceeded forth from the mouth of a Jew; and when it proceeded forth from the mouth of a Jew it contained the fulness of the gospel of the Lord, of whom the twelve apostles bear record; and they bear record according to the truth which is in the Lamb of God.

25. Wherefore, these things go forth from the Jews in purity unto the Gentiles, according to the truth which is in God.

26. And after they go forth by the hand of the twelve apostles of the Lamb, from the Jews unto the Gentiles, thou seest the formation of that great and abominable church, which is most

abominable above all other churches; for behold, they have taken away from the gospel of the Lamb many parts which are plain and most precious; and also many covenants of the Lord have they taken away.

27. And all this have they done that they might pervert the right ways of the Lord, that they might blind the eyes and harden the hearts of the children of men.

28. Wherefore, thou seest that after the book hath gone forth through the hands of the great and abominable church, that there are many plain and precious things taken away from the book, which is the book of the Lamb of God.

29. And after these plain and precious things were taken away it goeth forth unto all the nations of the Gentiles; and after it goeth forth unto all the nations of the Gentiles, yea, even across the many waters which thou hast seen with the Gentiles which have gone forth out of captivity, thou seest—because of the many plain and precious things which have been taken out of the book, which were plain unto the understanding of the children of men, according to the plainness which is in the Lamb of God—because of these things which are taken away out of the gospel of the Lamb, an exceedingly great many do stumble, yea, insomuch that Satan hath great power over them.

30. Nevertheless, thou beholdest that the Gentiles who have gone forth out of captivity, and have been lifted up by the power of God above all other nations, upon the face of the land which is choice above all other lands, which is the land that the Lord God hath covenanted with thy father that his seed should have for the land of their inheritance; wherefore, thou seest that the Lord God will not suffer that the Gentiles will utterly destroy the mixture of thy seed, which are among thy brethren.

31. Neither will he suffer that the Gentiles shall destroy the seed of thy brethren.

32. Neither will the Lord God suffer that the Gentiles shall forever remain in that awful state of blindness, which thou beholdest they are in, because of the plain and most precious parts of the gospel of the Lamb which have been kept back by that abominable church, whose formation thou hast seen.

33. Wherefore saith the Lamb of God: I will be merciful unto the Gentiles, unto the visiting of the remnant of the house of Israel in great judgment.

34. And it came to pass that the angel of the Lord spake unto me, saying: Behold, saith the Lamb of God, after I have visited the remnant of the house of Israel—and this remnant of whom I speak is the seed of thy father—wherefore, after I have visited them in judgment, and smitten them by the hand of the Gentiles, and after the Gentiles do stumble exceedingly, because of the most plain and precious parts of the gospel of the Lamb which have been kept back by that abominable church, which is the mother of harlots, saith the Lamb—I will be merciful unto the Gentiles in that day, insomuch that I will bring forth unto them, in mine own power, much of my gospel, which shall be plain and precious, saith the Lamb.

35. For, behold, saith the Lamb: I will manifest myself unto thy seed, that they shall write many things which I shall minister unto them, which shall be plain and precious; and after thy seed shall be destroyed, and dwindle in unbelief, and also the seed of thy brethren, behold, these things shall be hid up, to come forth unto the Gentiles, by the gift and power of the Lamb.

36. And in them shall be written my gospel, saith the Lamb, and my rock and my salvation.

37. And blessed are they who shall seek to bring forth my Zion

at that day, for they shall have the gift and the power of the Holy Ghost; and if they endure unto the end they shall be lifted up at the last day, and shall be saved in the everlasting kingdom of the Lamb; and whoso shall publish peace, yea, tidings of great joy, how beautiful upon the mountains shall they be.

38. And it came to pass that I beheld the remnant of the seed of my brethren, and also the book of the Lamb of God, which had proceeded forth from the mouth of the Jew, that it came forth from the Gentiles unto the remnant of the seed of my brethren.

39. And after it had come forth unto them I beheld other books, which came forth by the power of the Lamb, from the Gentiles unto them, unto the convincing of the Gentiles and the remnant of the seed of my brethren, and also the Jews who were scattered upon all the face of the earth, that the records of the prophets and of the twelve apostles of the Lamb are true.

40. And the angel spake unto me, saying: These last records, which thou hast seen among the Gentiles, shall establish the truth of the first, which are of the twelve apostles of the Lamb, and shall make known the plain and precious things which have been taken away from them; and shall make known to all kindreds, tongues, and people, that the Lamb of God is the Son of the Eternal Father, and the Savior of the world; and that all men must come unto him, or they cannot be saved.

41. And they must come according to the words which shall be established by the mouth of the Lamb; and the words of the Lamb shall be made known in the records of thy seed, as well as in the records of the twelve apostles of the Lamb; wherefore they both shall be established in one; for there is one God and one Shepherd over all the earth.

42. And the time cometh that he shall manifest himself unto all nations, both unto the Jews and also unto the Gentiles; and

after he has manifested himself unto the Jews and also unto the Gentiles, then he shall manifest himself unto the Gentiles and also unto the Jews, and the last shall be first, and the first shall be last.

1 Nephi 14

1. And it shall come to pass, that if the Gentiles shall hearken unto the Lamb of God in that day that he shall manifest himself unto them in word, and also in power, in very deed, unto the taking away of their stumbling blocks—

2. And harden not their hearts against the Lamb of God, they shall be numbered among the seed of thy father; yea, they shall be numbered among the house of Israel; and they shall be a blessed people upon the promised land forever; they shall be no more brought down into captivity; and the house of Israel shall no more be confounded.

3. And that great pit, which hath been digged for them by that great and abominable church, which was founded by the devil and his children, that he might lead away the souls of men down to hell—yea, that great pit which hath been digged for the destruction of men shall be filled by those who digged it, unto their utter destruction, saith the Lamb of God; not the destruction of the soul, save it be the casting of it into that hell which hath no end.

4. For behold, this is according to the captivity of the devil, and also according to the justice of God, upon all those who will work wickedness and abomination before him.

5. And it came to pass that the angel spake unto me, Nephi, saying: Thou hast beheld that if the Gentiles repent it shall be well with them; and thou also knowest concerning the covenants of the Lord unto the house of Israel; and thou also hast heard that whoso repenteth not must perish.

6. Therefore, wo be unto the Gentiles if it so be that they harden their hearts against the Lamb of God.

7. For the time cometh, saith the Lamb of God, that I will work a great and a marvelous work among the children of men; a work which shall be everlasting, either on the one hand or on the other—either to the convincing of them unto peace and life eternal, or unto the deliverance of them to the hardness of their hearts and the blindness of their minds unto their being brought down into captivity, and also into destruction, both temporally and spiritually, according to the captivity of the devil, of which I have spoken.

8. And it came to pass that when the angel had spoken these words, he said unto me: Rememberest thou the covenants of the Father unto the house of Israel? I said unto him, Yea.

9. And it came to pass that he said unto me: Look, and behold that great and abominable church, which is the mother of abomi-nations, whose founder is the devil.

10. And he said unto me: Behold there are save two churches only; the one is the church of the Lamb of God, and the other is the church of the devil; wherefore, whoso belongeth not to the church of the Lamb of God belongeth to that great church, which is the mother of abominations; and she is the whore of all the earth.

11. And it came to pass that I looked and beheld the whore of all the earth, and she sat upon many waters; and she had domin-ion over all the earth, among all nations, kindreds, tongues, and people.

12. And it came to pass that I beheld the church of the Lamb of God, and its numbers were few, because of the wickedness and abominations of the whore who sat upon many waters; neverthe-less, I beheld that the church of the Lamb, who were the saints of

God, were also upon all the face of the earth; and their dominions upon the face of the earth were small, because of the wickedness of the great whore whom I saw.

13. And it came to pass that I beheld that the great mother of abominations did gather together multitudes upon the face of all the earth, among all the nations of the Gentiles, to fight against the Lamb of God.

14. And it came to pass that I, Nephi, beheld the power of the Lamb of God, that it descended upon the saints of the church of the Lamb, and upon the covenant people of the Lord, who were scattered upon all the face of the earth; and they were armed with righteousness and with the power of God in great glory.

15. And it came to pass that I beheld that the wrath of God was poured out upon that great and abominable church, insomuch that there were wars and rumors of wars among all the nations and kindreds of the earth.

16. And as there began to be wars and rumors of wars among all the nations which belonged to the mother of abominations, the angel spake unto me, saying: Behold, the wrath of God is upon the mother of harlots; and behold, thou seest all these things—

17. And when the day cometh that the wrath of God is poured out upon the mother of harlots, which is the great and abominable church of all the earth, whose founder is the devil, then, at that day, the work of the Father shall commence, in preparing the way for the fulfilling of his covenants, which he hath made to his people who are of the house of Israel.

18. And it came to pass that the angel spake unto me, saying: Look!

19. And I looked and beheld a man, and he was dressed in a white robe.

20. And the angel said unto me: Behold one of the twelve apostles of the Lamb.

21. Behold, he shall see and write the remainder of these things; yea, and also many things which have been.

22. And he shall also write concerning the end of the world.

23. Wherefore, the things which he shall write are just and true; and behold they are written in the book which thou beheld proceeding out of the mouth of the Jew; and at the time they proceeded out of the mouth of the Jew, or, at the time the book proceeded out of the mouth of the Jew, the things which were written were plain and pure, and most precious and easy to the understanding of all men.

24. And behold, the things which this apostle of the Lamb shall write are many things which thou hast seen; and behold, the remainder shalt thou see.

25. But the things which thou shalt see hereafter thou shalt not write; for the Lord God hath ordained the apostle of the Lamb of God that he should write them.

26. And also others who have been, to them hath he shown all things, and they have written them; and they are sealed up to come forth in their purity, according to the truth which is in the Lamb, in the own due time of the Lord, unto the house of Israel.

27. And I, Nephi, heard and bear record, that the name of the apostle of the Lamb was John, according to the word of the angel.

28. And behold, I, Nephi, am forbidden that I should write the remainder of the things which I saw and heard; wherefore the things which I have written sufficeth me; and I have written but a small part of the things which I saw.

29. And I bear record that I saw the things which my father saw, and the angel of the Lord did make them known unto me.

30. And now I make an end of speaking concerning the things which I saw while I was carried away in the spirit; and if all the things which I saw are not written, the things which I have written are true. And thus it is. Amen.

That We May Always Have His Spirit to Be with Us

From *Ensign,* May 2006, 28–31

Baptism by immersion for the remission of sins "is the introductory ordinance of the gospel" of Jesus Christ and must be preceded by faith in the Savior and by sincere and complete repentance. "Baptism in water . . . must be followed by baptism of the Spirit in order to be complete" (see Bible Dictionary, "Baptism," 618). As the Savior taught Nicodemus, "Except a man be born of water and of the Spirit, he cannot enter into the kingdom of God" (John 3:5). This message focuses on the baptism of the Spirit and the blessings that flow from the companionship of the Holy Ghost.

The Ordinance of and Covenant Associated with Baptism

As each of us was baptized, we entered into a solemn covenant with our Heavenly Father. A covenant is an agreement between God and His children upon the earth, and it is important to understand that God determines the conditions of all gospel covenants. You and I do not decide the nature or elements of a covenant. Rather, exercising our moral agency, we accept the terms and requirements of a covenant as our Eternal Father has established them (see Bible Dictionary, "Covenant," 651).

The saving ordinance of baptism must be administered by one who has proper authority from God. The fundamental conditions of the covenant into which we entered in the waters of baptism are these: we witnessed that we were willing to take upon ourselves the name of Jesus Christ, that we would always remember Him, and that we would keep His commandments. The promised blessing for honoring this covenant is *that we may always have His Spirit to be with us* (see Doctrine and Covenants 20:77). In other words, baptism by water leads to the authorized opportunity for the constant companionship of the third member of the Godhead.

Confirmation and the Baptism of the Spirit

Following our baptism, each of us had hands placed upon his or her head by those with priesthood authority and was confirmed a member of The Church of Jesus Christ of Latter-day Saints, and the Holy Ghost was conferred upon us (see Doctrine and Covenants 49:14). The statement "receive the Holy Ghost" in our confirmation was a directive to strive for the baptism of the Spirit.

The Prophet Joseph Smith taught: "You might as well baptize a bag of sand as a man, if not done in view of the remission of sins and getting of the Holy Ghost. Baptism by water is but half a baptism, and is good for nothing without the other half—that is, the baptism of the Holy Ghost" (in *History of the Church,* 5:499). We were baptized by immersion in water for the remission of sins. We must also be baptized by and immersed in the Spirit of the Lord, "and then cometh a remission of your sins by fire and by the Holy Ghost" (2 Nephi 31:17).

As we gain experience with the Holy Ghost, we learn that the intensity with which we feel the Spirit's influence is not always the same. Strong, dramatic spiritual impressions do not come to us frequently. Even as we strive to be faithful and obedient, there simply are times when the direction, assurance, and peace of the Spirit are not readily recognizable in our lives. In fact, the Book of Mormon describes faithful Lamanites who "were baptized with fire and with the Holy Ghost, and they knew it not" (3 Nephi 9:20).

The influence of the Holy Ghost is described in the scriptures as "a still small voice" (1 Kings 19:12; see also 3 Nephi 11:3) and a "voice of perfect mildness" (Helaman 5:30). Thus, the Spirit of the Lord usually communicates with us in ways that are quiet, delicate, and subtle.

Withdrawing Ourselves from the Spirit of the Lord

In our individual study and classroom instruction, we repeatedly emphasize the importance of recognizing the inspiration and promptings we receive from the Spirit of the Lord. And such an approach is correct and useful. We should seek diligently to recognize and respond to promptings as they come to us. However, an important aspect of baptism by the Spirit may frequently be overlooked in our spiritual development.

We should also endeavor to discern when we "withdraw [ourselves] from the Spirit of the Lord, that it may have no place in [us] to guide [us] in wisdom's paths that [we] may be blessed, prospered, and preserved" (Mosiah 2:36). Precisely because the promised blessing is *that we may always have His Spirit to be with us,* we should attend to and learn from the choices and influences that separate us from the Holy Spirit.

The standard is clear. If something we think, see, hear, or do distances us from the Holy Ghost, then we should stop thinking, seeing, hearing, or doing that thing. If that which is intended to entertain, for example, alienates us from the Holy Spirit, then certainly that type of entertainment is not for us. Because the Spirit cannot abide that which is vulgar, crude, or immodest, then clearly such things are not for us. Because we estrange the Spirit of the Lord when we engage in activities we know we should shun, then such things definitely are not for us.

I recognize we are fallen men and women living in a mortal world and that we might not have the presence of the Holy Ghost with us every second of every minute of every hour of every day. However, the Holy Ghost can tarry with us much, if not most, of the time—and certainly the Spirit can be with us more than it is not with us. As we become ever more immersed in the Spirit of the Lord, we should strive to recognize impressions when they come and the influences or events that cause us to withdraw ourselves from the Holy Ghost.

Taking "the Holy Spirit for [our] guide" (Doctrine and Covenants 45:57) is possible and is essential for our spiritual growth and survival in an increasingly wicked world. Sometimes as Latter-day Saints we talk and act as though recognizing the influence of the Holy Ghost in our lives is the rare or exceptional event. We should remember, however, that the covenant promise is *that we may always have His Spirit to be with us.* This supernal blessing applies to every single member of the Church who has been baptized, confirmed, and instructed to "receive the Holy Ghost."

The Liahona as a Type and Shadow for Our Day

In our day the Book of Mormon is the primary source to which we should turn for help in learning how to invite the constant companionship of the Holy Ghost. The description in the Book of Mormon of the Liahona, the director or compass used by Lehi and his family in their journey in the wilderness, specifically was included in the record as a type and a shadow for our day and as an essential lesson about what we should do to enjoy the blessings of the Holy Ghost.

As we strive to align our attitudes and actions with righteousness, then the Holy Ghost becomes for us today what the Liahona was for Lehi and his family in their day. The very factors that caused the Liahona to work for Lehi will likewise invite the Holy Ghost into our lives. And the very factors that caused the Liahona not to work anciently will likewise cause us to withdraw ourselves from the Holy Ghost today.

The Liahona: Purposes and Principles

As we study and ponder the purposes of the Liahona and the principles by which it operated, I testify that we will receive inspiration suited to our individual and family circumstances and needs. We can and will be blessed with ongoing direction from the Holy Ghost.

The Liahona was prepared by the Lord and given to Lehi and his family after they left Jerusalem and were traveling in the wilderness (see Alma 37:38; Doctrine and Covenants 17:1). This compass or director pointed the way that Lehi and his caravan should go (see 1 Nephi 16:10), even "a straight course to the promised land" (Alma 37:44). The pointers in the Liahona operated "according to the faith and diligence and heed" (1 Nephi 16:28) of the travelers and failed to work when family members were contentious, rude, slothful, or forgetful (see 1 Nephi 18:12, 21; Alma 37:41, 43).

The compass also provided a means whereby Lehi and his family could obtain greater "understanding concerning the ways of the Lord" (1 Nephi 16:29). Thus, the primary purposes of the Liahona were to provide both direction and instruction during a long and demanding journey. The director was a physical instrument that served as an outward indicator of their inner spiritual standing before God. It worked according to the principles of faith and diligence.

Just as Lehi was blessed in ancient times, each of us in this day has been given a spiritual compass that can direct and instruct us during our mortal journey. The Holy Ghost was conferred upon you and me as we came out of the world and into the Savior's Church through baptism and confirmation. By the authority of the holy priesthood we were confirmed as members of the Church and admonished to seek for the constant companionship of "the Spirit of truth; whom the world cannot receive, because it seeth him not, neither knoweth him: but ye know him; for he dwelleth with you, and shall be in you" (John 14:17).

As we each press forward along the pathway of life, we receive direction from the Holy Ghost just as Lehi was directed through the Liahona. "For behold, again I say unto you that if ye will enter in by the way, and receive the Holy Ghost, it will show unto you all things what ye should do" (2 Nephi 32:5).

The Holy Ghost operates in our lives precisely as the Liahona did for Lehi and his family, according to our faith and diligence and heed.

"Let virtue garnish thy thoughts unceasingly; then shall thy confidence wax strong in the presence of God. . . .

"The Holy Ghost shall be thy constant companion, and thy scepter an unchanging scepter of righteousness and truth" (Doctrine and Covenants 121:45–46).

And the Holy Ghost provides for us today the means whereby we can receive, "by small and simple things" (Alma 37:6), increased understanding about the ways of the Lord: "But the Comforter, which is the Holy Ghost, whom the Father will send in my name, he shall teach you all things, and bring all things to your remembrance, whatsoever I have said unto you" (John 14:26).

The Spirit of the Lord can be our guide and will bless us with direction, instruction, and spiritual protection during our mortal journey. We invite the Holy Ghost into our lives through meaningful personal and family prayer, feasting upon the words of Christ, diligent and exacting obedience, faithfulness and honoring of covenants, and through virtue, humility, and service. And we steadfastly should avoid things that are immodest, coarse, crude, sinful, or evil that cause us to withdraw ourselves from the Holy Ghost.

We also invite the ongoing companionship of the Holy Ghost as we worthily partake of the sacrament each Sabbath day: "And that thou mayest more fully keep thyself unspotted from the world, thou shalt go to the house of prayer and offer up thy sacraments upon my holy day" (Doctrine and Covenants 59:9).

Through the ordinance of the sacrament we renew our baptismal covenant and can receive and retain a remission of our sins (see Mosiah 4:12, 26). In addition, we are reminded on a weekly basis of the promise *that we may always have His Spirit to be with us.* As we then strive to keep ourselves clean and unspotted from the world, we become worthy vessels in whom the Spirit of the Lord can always dwell.

May each of us so live *that we may always have His Spirit to be with us* and thereby qualify for the blessings of direction, instruction, and protection that are essential in these latter days.

Receive the Holy Ghost

From *Ensign,* November 2010, 94–97

The Gift of the Holy Ghost

In December of 1839, while in Washington, D.C., to seek redress for the wrongs done to the Missouri Saints, Joseph Smith and Elias Higbee wrote to Hyrum Smith: "In our interview with the President [of the United States], he interrogated us wherein we differed in our religion from the other religions of the day. Brother Joseph said we differed in mode of baptism, and the gift of the Holy Ghost by the laying on of hands. We considered that all other considerations were contained in the gift of the Holy Ghost" (*Teachings: Joseph Smith,* 97).

The Holy Ghost is the third member of the Godhead; He is a personage of spirit and bears witness of all truth. In the scriptures the Holy Ghost is referred to as the Comforter (see John 14:16–27; Moroni 8:26), a teacher (see John 14:26; Doctrine and Covenants 50:14), and a revelator (see 2 Nephi 32:5). Revelations from the Father and the Son are conveyed through the Holy Ghost. He is the messenger for and the witness of the Father and the Son.

The Holy Ghost is manifested to men and women on the earth both as the power and as the gift of the Holy Ghost. The power can come upon a person before baptism; it is the convincing witness that Jesus Christ is our Savior and Redeemer. Through the power of the Holy Ghost, sincere investigators can acquire a conviction of the truthfulness of the Savior's gospel, of the Book of Mormon, of the reality of the Restoration, and of the prophetic calling of Joseph Smith.

The gift of the Holy Ghost is bestowed only after proper and authorized baptism and by the laying on of hands by those holding the Melchizedek Priesthood. The Lord declared:

"Yea, repent and be baptized, every one of you, for a remission of your sins; yea, be baptized even by water, and then cometh the baptism of fire and of the Holy Ghost. . . .

"And whoso having faith you shall confirm in my church, by the laying on of the hands, and I will bestow the gift of the Holy Ghost upon them" (Doctrine and Covenants 33:11, 15).

The Apostle Paul made this practice clear to the Ephesians when he asked:

"Have ye received the Holy Ghost since ye believed? And they said unto him, We have not so much as heard whether there be any Holy Ghost.

"And he said unto them, Unto what then were ye baptized? And they said, Unto John's baptism.

"Then said Paul, John verily baptized with the baptism of repentance, saying unto the people, that they should believe on him which should come after him, that is, on Christ Jesus.

"When they heard this, they were baptized in the name of the Lord Jesus.

"And when Paul had laid his hands upon them, the Holy Ghost came on them" (Acts 19:2–6).

Baptism by immersion is "the introductory ordinance of the gospel, and must be followed by baptism of the Spirit in order to be complete" (Bible Dictionary, "Baptism"). The Prophet Joseph Smith explained that "baptism is a holy ordinance preparatory to the reception of the Holy Ghost; it is the channel and key by which the Holy Ghost will be administered. The Gift of the Holy Ghost by the laying on of hands, cannot be received through the medium of any other principle than the principle of righteousness" (*Teachings: Joseph Smith*, 95–96).

The ordinance of confirming a new member of the Church and bestowing the gift of the Holy Ghost is both simple and profound. Worthy Melchizedek Priesthood holders place their hands upon the head of an individual and call him or her by name. Then, by the authority of the holy priesthood and in the name of the Savior, the individual is confirmed a member of The Church of Jesus Christ of Latter-day Saints, and this important phrase is uttered: "Receive the Holy Ghost."

The simplicity of this ordinance may cause us to overlook its significance. These four words—"Receive the Holy Ghost"—are not a passive pronouncement; rather, they constitute a priesthood injunction—an authoritative admonition to act and not simply to be acted upon (see 2 Nephi 2:26). The Holy Ghost does not become operative in our lives merely because hands are placed upon our heads and those four important words are spoken. As we receive this ordinance, each of us accepts a sacred and ongoing responsibility to desire, to seek, to work, and to so live that we indeed "receive the Holy Ghost" and its attendant spiritual gifts. "For what doth it profit a man if a gift is bestowed upon him, and he receive not the gift? Behold, he rejoices not in that which is given unto him, neither rejoices in him who is the giver of the gift" (Doctrine and Covenants 88:33).

What should we do to make this authorized admonition to seek for the companionship of the third member of the Godhead an ongoing reality? Let me suggest that we need to (1) sincerely desire to receive the Holy Ghost, (2) appropriately invite the Holy Ghost into our lives, and (3) faithfully obey God's commandments.

Sincerely Desire

We first should desire, yearn for, and seek the companionship of the Holy Ghost. You and I can learn a great lesson about righteous desires from the faithful disciples of the Master described in the Book of Mormon:

"And the twelve did teach the multitude; and behold, they did cause that the multitude should kneel down upon the face of the earth, and should pray unto the Father in the name of Jesus. . . .

"And they did pray for that which they most desired; and they desired that the Holy Ghost should be given unto them" (3 Nephi 19:6, 9).

Do we likewise remember to pray earnestly and consistently for that which we should most desire, even the Holy Ghost? Or do we become distracted by the cares of the world and the routine of daily living and take for granted or even neglect this most valuable of all gifts? Receiving the Holy Ghost starts with our sincere and constant desire for His companionship in our lives.

Appropriately Invite

We more readily receive and recognize the Spirit of the Lord as we appropriately invite Him into our lives. We cannot compel, coerce, or command the Holy Ghost. Rather, we should invite Him into our lives with the same gentleness and tenderness by which He entreats us (see Doctrine and Covenants 42:14).

Our invitations for the companionship of the Holy Ghost occur in many ways: through the making and keeping of covenants; by praying sincerely as individuals and families; by searching the scriptures diligently; through strengthening appropriate relationships with family members and friends; by seeking after virtuous thoughts, actions, and language; and by worshipping in our homes, in the holy temple, and at church. Conversely, casualness about or the breaking of covenants and commitments, failing to pray and study the scriptures, and inappropriate thoughts, actions, and language cause the Spirit to withdraw from or to avoid us altogether.

As King Benjamin taught his people, "And now, I say unto you, my brethren, that after ye have known and have been taught all these things, if ye should transgress and go contrary to that which has been spoken, that ye do withdraw yourselves from the Spirit of the Lord, that it may have no place in you to guide you in wisdom's paths that ye may be blessed, prospered, and preserved" (Mosiah 2:36).

Faithfully Obey

Faithfully obeying God's commandments is essential to receiving the Holy Ghost. We are reminded of this truth each week as we listen to the sacrament prayers and worthily partake of the bread and water. As we pledge our willingness to take upon ourselves the name of Jesus Christ, to always remember Him, and to keep His commandments, we are promised that we may always have His Spirit to be with us (see Doctrine and Covenants 20:77). Thus, everything the Savior's gospel teaches us to do and become is intended to bless us with the companionship of the Holy Ghost.

Consider the reasons we pray and study the scriptures. Yes, we yearn to communicate in prayer with Heavenly Father in the name of His Son. And yes, we desire to obtain the light and knowledge available in the standard works. But please remember that these holy habits primarily are ways whereby we always remember

Heavenly Father and His Beloved Son and are prerequisites to the ongoing companionship of the Holy Ghost.

Reflect on the reasons we worship in the house of the Lord and in our Sabbath meetings. Yes, we serve our kindred dead in the temple—and our families and friends in the wards and branches in which we live. And yes, we enjoy the righteous sociality we find among our brothers and sisters. But we primarily gather together in unity to seek the blessings of and instruction from the Holy Ghost.

Praying, studying, gathering, worshipping, serving, and obeying are not isolated and independent items on a lengthy gospel checklist of things to do. Rather, each of these righteous practices is an important element in an overarching spiritual quest to fulfill the mandate to receive the Holy Ghost. The commandments from God we obey and the inspired counsel from Church leaders we follow principally focus upon obtaining the companionship of the Spirit. Fundamentally, all gospel teachings and activities are centered on coming unto Christ by receiving the Holy Ghost in our lives.

You and I should strive to become like the stripling warriors described in the Book of Mormon, who did "perform every word of command with exactness; yea, and even according to their faith it was done unto them. . . .

" . . . And they are strict to remember the Lord their God from day to day; yea, they do observe to keep his statutes, and his judgments, and his commandments continually" (Alma 57:21; 58:40).

Testimony

The Lord has declared that The Church of Jesus Christ of Latter-day Saints is "the only true and living church upon the face of the whole earth" (Doctrine and Covenants 1:30). This restored Church is true because it is the Savior's Church; He is "the way, the truth, and the life" (John 14:6). And it is a living church because of the workings and gifts of the Holy Ghost. How blessed we are to live at a time when the priesthood is upon the earth and we can receive the Holy Ghost.

Several years after the Prophet Joseph Smith was martyred, he appeared to President Brigham Young and shared this timeless counsel: "Tell the people to be humble and faithful and [be] sure to keep the Spirit of the Lord and it will lead them right. Be careful and not turn away the small still voice; it will teach [you what] to do and where to go; it will yield the fruits of the kingdom. Tell the brethren to keep their hearts open to conviction so that when the Holy Ghost comes to them, their hearts will be ready to receive it. They can tell the Spirit of the Lord from all other spirits. It will whisper peace and joy to their souls, and it will take malice, hatred, envying, strife, and all evil from their hearts; and their whole desire will be to do good, bring forth righteousness, and build up the kingdom of God. Tell the brethren if they will follow the Spirit of the Lord they will go right" (*Teachings: Joseph Smith,* 98).

I pray we will sincerely desire and appropriately invite the Holy Ghost into our daily lives. I also pray each of us will faithfully obey God's commandments and in reality receive the Holy Ghost. I promise the blessings described by the Prophet Joseph Smith to Brigham Young are applicable to and attainable by every individual.

Quick to Observe

From *Ensign*, December 2006, 30–36

In October 1987 Elder Marvin J. Ashton, a member of the Quorum of the Twelve Apostles, spoke in general conference about spiritual gifts. I recall with fondness the impact his message had upon me at that time, and the things he taught then continue to influence me today. In his message Elder Ashton detailed and described a number of less conspicuous spiritual gifts—attributes and abilities that many of us might not have considered being spiritual gifts. For example, Elder Ashton highlighted the gifts of asking; of listening; of hearing and using a still, small voice; of being able to weep; of avoiding contention; of being agreeable; of avoiding vain repetition; of seeking that which is righteous; of looking to God for guidance; of being a disciple; of caring for others; of being able to ponder; of bearing mighty testimony; and of receiving the Holy Ghost (see "There Are Many Gifts," 20).

Another seemingly simple and perhaps underappreciated spiritual gift—the capacity of being "quick to observe" (Mormon 1:2)—is vitally important for you and for me in the world in which we do now and will yet live.

The Spiritual Gift of Being Quick to Observe

All of us have learned important lessons from the central characters in the Book of Mormon. As we read about and study the lives of Nephi, Laman, Alma, King Noah, Moroni, and many others, we discover things we should and should not do, and we realize more completely the kinds of people we should and should not become.

In my study of the Book of Mormon I have been especially impressed with a particular description of Mormon, the principal compiler of the Nephite record. The specific depiction of this noble prophet to which I would direct our attention is contained in the first five verses of the first chapter of Mormon:

"And now I, Mormon, make a record of the things which I have both seen and heard, and call it the Book of Mormon.

"And about the time that Ammaron hid up the records unto the Lord, he came unto me, (I being about ten years of age . . .) and Ammaron said unto me: I perceive that thou art a sober child, and art *quick to observe;*

"Therefore, when ye are about twenty and four years old I would that ye should remember the things that ye have observed concerning this people; . . .

"And behold, . . . ye shall engrave on the plates of Nephi all the things that ye have observed concerning this people.

"And I, Mormon, . . . remembered the things which Ammaron commanded me" (Mormon 1:1–5; emphasis added).

Please note that the root word *observe* is used three times in these verses. And Mormon, even in his youth, is described as being "quick to observe." As you study and learn and grow, I hope you also are learning about and becoming quick to observe. Your future success and happiness will in large measure be determined by this spiritual capacity.

Please consider the significance of this important spiritual gift. As used in the scriptures, the word *observe* has two primary uses. One use denotes "to look" or "to see" or "to notice"—as we learn in

Isaiah 42:20: "Seeing many things, but thou *observest* not; opening the ears, but he heareth not" (emphasis added).

The second use of the word *observe* suggests "to obey" or "to keep"—as is evident in the Doctrine and Covenants: "But blessed are they who have kept the covenant and *observed* the commandment, for they shall obtain mercy" (Doctrine and Covenants 54:6; emphasis added).

Thus when we are quick to observe, we promptly look or notice and obey. Both of these fundamental elements—looking and obeying—are essential to being quick to observe. And the prophet Mormon is an impressive example of this gift in action.

I now want to present several examples of the lessons that can be learned when you and I are blessed to be quick to observe.

I have a dear friend who served as a stake president. The patriarch in the stake over which he presided had experienced some health challenges and was unable to perform in his calling. The ailing patriarch had difficulty moving about and dressing and caring for himself, and his strength was limited. One Sabbath afternoon this good stake president visited the home of the patriarch to encourage him and check on his well-being. As the stake president entered the home, he found the patriarch dressed in his suit and white shirt and tie, sitting in a recliner in the front room. The stake president greeted the dear patriarch and, knowing how hard it must have been to dress himself, graciously suggested to the patriarch that it was not necessary for him to get dressed up on the Sabbath or to meet visitors. In a kind but firm voice, the patriarch reproved the stake president and said, "Don't you know that this is the only way I have left to show the Lord how much I love Him?"

The stake president was quick to observe. He both heard and felt the lesson, and he applied it. Reverence for the Sabbath day and the importance of respect and appropriate demeanor and dress took on added importance in the ministry of the stake president. The spiritual ability to see, hear, remember, and act upon that lesson was a great blessing in his life—and in the lives of many others.

Before attending her sacrament meetings, Sister Bednar frequently prays for the spiritual eyes to see those who have a need. Often as she observes the brothers and sisters and children in the congregation, she will feel a spiritual nudge to visit with or make a phone call to a particular person. And when Sister Bednar receives such an impression, she promptly responds and obeys. It often is the case that as soon as the "amen" is spoken in the benediction, she will talk with a teenager or hug a sister or, upon returning home, immediately pick up the phone and make a call. As long as I have known Sister Bednar, people have marveled at her capacity to discern and respond to their needs. Often they will ask her, "How did you know?" The spiritual gift of being quick to observe has enabled her to see and to act promptly and has been a great blessing in the lives of many people.

Sister Bednar and I are acquainted with a returned missionary who had dated a special young woman for a period of time. He cared for her very much, and he was desirous of making his relationship with her more serious. He was considering and hoping for engagement and marriage. This relationship was developing during the time that President Hinckley counseled the Relief Society sisters and young women of the Church to wear only one earring in each ear.

The young man waited patiently over a period of time for the young woman to remove her extra earrings, but she did not take them out. This was a valuable piece of information for this young man, and he felt unsettled about her nonresponsiveness to a prophet's pleading. For this and other reasons, he ultimately stopped dating the young woman, because he was looking for an eternal companion who had the courage to promptly and quietly obey the counsel of the prophet in all things and at all times. The young man was quick to observe that the young woman was not quick to observe.

I presume that some of you might have difficulty with my last example. You may believe the young man was too judgmental or that basing an eternally important decision, even in part, upon such a supposedly minor issue is silly or fanatical. Perhaps you are bothered because the example focuses upon a young woman who failed to respond to prophetic counsel instead of upon a young man. I simply invite you to consider and ponder the power of being quick to observe and what was actually observed in the case I just described. The issue was not earrings!

One final example. I have long been fascinated by the nature of the interaction between the Spirit of the Lord and Nephi found in chapters 11 through 14 of 1 Nephi. Nephi desired to see and hear and know the things his father, Lehi, had seen in the vision of the tree of life (see 1 Nephi 8). In chapters 11 through 14 the Holy Ghost assisted Nephi in learning about the nature and meaning of his father's vision. Interestingly, thirteen times in these chapters the Spirit of the Lord directed Nephi to "look" as a fundamental feature of the learning process. Nephi repeatedly was counseled to look, and because he was quick to observe, he beheld the tree of life (see 1 Nephi 11:8), the mother of the Savior (see 1 Nephi 11:20), the rod of iron (see 1 Nephi 11:25), and the Lamb of God, the Son of the Eternal Father (see 1 Nephi 11:21).

I have described only a few of the spiritually significant things Nephi saw. You may want to study these chapters in greater depth and learn from and about Nephi's learning. As you study and ponder, please keep in mind that Nephi would not have seen what he desired to see, would not have known what he needed to know, and could not have done what he ultimately needed to do if he had not been quick to observe. That same truth applies to you and to me!

Quick to observe. Prompt to watch and to obey. A simple gift that blesses us individually and in our families and extends blessings to so many other people. Each of us can and should strive to be worthy of this significant spiritual gift—even the capacity of being quick to observe.

The Importance of Being Quick to Observe

Let me now address the question of why the spiritual gift of being quick to observe is so vital for us in the world in which we do now and will yet live. Simply stated, being quick to observe is an antecedent to and is linked with the spiritual gift of discernment. And for you and for me, discernment is a light of protection and direction in a world that grows increasingly dark.

Much like faith precedes the miracle, much like baptism by water comes before the baptism by fire, much like gospel milk should be digested before gospel meat, much like clean hands can lead to a pure heart, and much like the ordinances of the Aaronic Priesthood are necessary before a person can receive the higher ordinances of the Melchizedek Priesthood, so being quick to observe is a prerequisite to and a preparation for the gift of discernment. We can hope to obtain that supernal gift of discernment and its light of protection and direction only if we are quick to observe— if we both look and obey.

President George Q. Cannon (1827–1901), who served as a counselor to four Presidents of the Church, taught powerfully about the gift of discernment:

"One of the gifts of the Gospel which the Lord has promised

to those who enter into covenant with Him is the gift of discerning of spirits—a gift which is not much thought of by many and probably seldom prayed for; yet it is a gift that is of exceeding value and one that should be enjoyed by every Latter-day Saint. . . .

"Now, the gift of discerning of spirits not only gives men and women who have it the power to discern the spirit with which others may be possessed or influenced, but it gives them the power to discern the spirit which influences themselves. They are able to detect a false spirit and also to know when the Spirit of God reigns within them. In private life this gift is of great importance to the Latter-day Saints. Possessing and exercising this gift they will not allow any evil influence to enter into their hearts or to prompt them in their thoughts, their words or their acts. They will repel it; and if perchance such a spirit should get possession of them, as soon as they witness its effects they will expel it or, in other words, refuse to be led or prompted by it" (*Gospel Truth,* 156–57).

Can we recognize how crucial this spiritual gift is in our lives today and how being quick to observe is a powerful invitation for the blessings of discernment?

President Stephen L Richards (1879–1959), who served as a counselor to President David O. McKay, has provided additional instruction about the nature and blessings of discernment:

"First, I mention the gift of discernment, embodying the power to discriminate . . . between right and wrong. I believe that this gift when highly developed arises largely out of an acute sensitivity to impressions—spiritual impressions, if you will—to read under the surface as it were, to detect hidden evil, and more importantly to find the good that may be concealed. The highest type of discernment is that which perceives in others and uncovers for them their better natures, the good inherent within them. . . .

" . . . *Every member in the restored Church of Christ could have this gift if he willed to do so.* He could not be deceived with the sophistries of the world. He could not be led astray by pseudo-prophets and subversive cults. Even the inexperienced would recognize false teachings, in a measure at least. . . . We ought to be grateful every day of our lives for this sense which keeps alive a conscience which constantly alerts us to the dangers inherent in wrongdoers and sin" (in Conference Report, April 1950, 162–63; emphasis added).

As we integrate the teachings of Presidents Cannon and Richards, we learn that the gift of discernment operates basically in four major ways.

First, as we "read under the surface," discernment helps us detect hidden error and evil in others.

Second, and more important, it helps us detect hidden errors and evil in ourselves. Thus the spiritual gift of discernment is not exclusively about discerning other people and situations, but, as President Cannon taught, it is also about discerning things as they really are within us.

Third, it helps us find and bring forth the good that may be concealed in others.

And fourth, it helps us find and bring forth the good that may be concealed in us. Oh, what a blessing and a source of protection and direction is the spiritual gift of discernment!

The teachings of Presidents Cannon and Richards concerning the power of discernment to detect hidden evil and to identify good that may be concealed become even more important to you and to me in light of a specific element of Lehi's vision. In the vision various groups of individuals were pressing forward that they might obtain the path which led unto the tree of life. The strait and narrow path came along by the rod of iron, even to the tree. The mist of darkness described in the vision represents the temptations of the devil that blind the eyes of the children of men and lead them into broad roads so that they are lost (see 1 Nephi 12:17).

Now please pay particular attention to verse 23 in 1 Nephi 8, and let us liken this scripture to our day and the challenges we face in an increasingly wicked world:

"And it came to pass that there arose a mist of darkness; yea, even an exceedingly great mist of darkness, insomuch that they who had commenced in the path did lose their way, that they wandered off and were lost."

I repeat again for emphasis the truth that discernment is a light of protection and direction in a world that grows increasingly dark. You and I can press forward safely and successfully through the mist of darkness and have a clear sense of spiritual direction. Discernment is so much more than recognizing right from wrong. It helps us distinguish the relevant from the irrelevant, the important from the unimportant, and the necessary from that which is merely nice.

The gift of discernment opens to us vistas that stretch far beyond what can be seen with natural eyes or heard with natural ears. Discerning is seeing with spiritual eyes and feeling with the heart—seeing and feeling the falsehood of an idea or the goodness in another person. Discerning is hearing with spiritual ears and feeling with the heart—hearing and feeling the unspoken concern in a statement or the truthfulness of a testimony or doctrine.

I frequently have heard President Boyd K. Packer, Acting President of the Quorum of the Twelve Apostles, counsel members and priesthood leaders, "If all you know is what you see with your natural eyes and hear with your natural ears, then you will not know very much." His observation should help all of us to appropriately desire and seek these spiritual gifts.

Observing and discerning also enable us to assist others who are seeking to obtain the path and who desire to press forward with steadfastness in Christ. Blessed with these spiritual gifts, we will not lose our way; we will not wander off; we will not be lost. And we can hope to obtain the supernal gift of discernment and its light of protection and direction only if we are quick to observe. As Alma taught his son Helaman, "See that ye take care of these sacred things, yea, see that ye look to God and live" (Alma 37:47).

I declare my special witness that Jesus is the Christ, our Redeemer and our Savior. I know that He lives. I invoke His blessing upon each of you—that you may desire to be and become quick to observe and truly discerning.

CHAPTER TWO

Knowledge, Understanding, and Intelligence

A hierarchy of importance exists among the things you and I can learn. Indeed, all information and knowledge are not equally important. The Apostle Paul taught this truth in his second epistle to Timothy as he warned that in the latter days many people would be "ever learning, and never able to come to the knowledge of the truth" (2 Timothy 3:7).

Many facts are helpful or merely interesting to know. Some knowledge is useful to learn and apply. But gospel truths are essential for us to understand and live if we are to become what our Heavenly Father yearns for us to become.

Knowledge

Generally, *knowledge* refers to facts, information, and abilities obtained through experience or education. Using the instrument of our physical bodies and our capacity to reflect and reason, we can gather and analyze facts, organize and interpret information, gain and learn from experience, and identify patterns and relationships.

Obtaining, creating, communicating, and applying knowledge are the overarching objectives of education.

Of the many types of knowledge that can be acquired, spiritual knowledge is the most important—both in mortality and eternity. The Prophet Joseph Smith repeatedly emphasized the importance of knowledge concerning the things of God.

"The principle of *knowledge* is the principle of salvation. This principle can be comprehended by the faithful and diligent; and every one that does not obtain *knowledge* sufficient to be saved will be condemned. The principle of salvation is given us through the *knowledge* of Jesus Christ" (*Teachings: Joseph Smith*, 212; emphasis added).

"*Knowledge* is necessary to life and godliness. Woe unto you priests and divines who preach that *knowledge* is not necessary unto life and salvation. . . . *Knowledge* is revelation. Hear, all ye brethren, this grand key: *knowledge* is the power of God unto salvation" (*Teachings: Joseph Smith*, 265; emphasis added).

"*Knowledge* does away with darkness, suspense and doubt; for these cannot exist where *knowledge* is. . . . In *knowledge* there is power. God has more power than all other beings, because He has greater *knowledge;* and hence He knows how to subject all other beings to Him. He has power over all" (*Teachings: Joseph Smith*, 265; emphasis added).

"A man is saved no faster than he gets *knowledge,* for if he does not get *knowledge,* he will be brought into captivity by some evil power in the other world, as evil spirits will have more *knowledge,* and consequently more power than many men who are on the earth. Hence it needs revelation to assist us, and give us *knowledge* of the things of God" (*Teachings: Joseph Smith*, 266; emphasis added).

"Truth is *knowledge* of things as they are, and as they were, and as they are to come" (Doctrine and Covenants 93:24; emphasis added).

"How long can rolling waters remain impure? What power shall stay the heavens? As well might man stretch forth his puny arm to stop the Missouri river in its decreed course, or to turn it up stream, as to hinder the Almighty from *pouring down knowledge* from heaven upon the heads of the Latter-day Saints" (Doctrine and Covenants 121:33; emphasis added).

"No power or influence can or ought to be maintained by virtue of the priesthood, only by persuasion, by long-suffering, by gentleness and meekness, and by love unfeigned;

"By kindness, and *pure knowledge,* which shall greatly enlarge the soul without hypocrisy, and without guile" (Doctrine and Covenants 121:41–42; emphasis added).

"And all saints who remember to keep and do these sayings, walking in obedience to the commandments, shall receive health in their navel and marrow to their bones;

"And shall find wisdom and great *treasures of knowledge,* even hidden treasures" (Doctrine and Covenants 89:18–19; emphasis added).

As explained in the *Lectures on Faith,* "For a man to lay down his all, his character and reputation, his honor, and applause, his good name among men, his houses, his lands, his brothers and sisters, his wife and children, and even his own life also—counting all things but filth and dross for the excellency of the *knowledge* of Jesus Christ—requires more than mere belief or supposition that he is doing the will of God; but *actual knowledge,* realizing that, when these sufferings are ended, he will enter into eternal rest, and be a partaker of the glory of God" (page 68; emphasis added).

And the Lord Himself declared clearly and concisely, "It is impossible for a man to be saved in ignorance" (Doctrine and Covenants 131:6).

Thus, a correct knowledge of the things of God is the vital cornerstone upon which the additional blessings of understanding and intelligence are built.

UNDERSTANDING

Understanding is the keystone that is erected upon the cornerstone of knowledge and precedes intelligence. Interestingly, the word *understanding* commonly is described in the scriptures in relation to the heart.

"Who hath put wisdom in the inward parts? or who hath given *understanding* to the *heart?*" (Job 38:36; emphasis added).

"My mouth shall speak of wisdom; and the meditation of my *heart* shall be of *understanding*" (Psalm 49:3; emphasis added).

"So that thou incline thine ear unto wisdom, and apply thine *heart* to *understanding*" (Proverbs 2:2; emphasis added).

"Ye have not applied your *hearts* to *understanding;* therefore, ye have not been wise" (Mosiah 12:27; emphasis added).

"Hearken unto me, and open your ears that ye may hear, and your *hearts* that ye may *understand,* and your minds that the mysteries of God may be unfolded to your view" (Mosiah 2:9; emphasis added).

"Now, we will compare the word unto a seed. Now, if ye give place, that a seed may be planted in your *heart,* behold, if it be a true seed, or a good seed, if ye do not cast it out by your unbelief, that ye will resist the Spirit of the Lord, behold, it will begin to swell within your breasts; and when you feel these swelling motions, ye will begin to say within yourselves—It must needs be that this is a good seed, or that the word is good, for it beginneth to enlarge my soul; yea, it beginneth to enlighten my *understanding,* yea, it beginneth to be delicious to me" (Alma 32:28; emphasis added).

"And the multitude did hear and do bear record; and their hearts were open and they did *understand* in their *hearts* the words which he prayed" (3 Nephi 19:33; emphasis added).

In these verses understanding is linked first and foremost to the heart. Clearly we must use our minds and our rational capacity; however, we are not explicitly counseled to apply our *minds,* but our *hearts,* in seeking for understanding. Perhaps the implication of the scriptures is that reason and "the arm of flesh" (Doctrine and Covenants 1:19) are not sufficient to engender true understanding. The word *understanding* as used in the scriptures does not refer solely or even primarily to intellectual or cognitive comprehension. Rather, when the Holy Ghost confirms in our hearts as true what we know in our minds, understanding occurs.

We begin to understand and experience a mighty change of heart as testimony and conviction move from our heads to our hearts. Thoughts and feelings put into our hearts by the Holy Ghost (see Doctrine and Covenants 100:5–8; 8:2) are a result of the spiritual gift of revelation. Understanding, then, is a revealed conclusion and a spiritual gift.

A confirming spiritual witness in our hearts concerning the truth of what we have come to know in our minds is obtained through the process of revelation. The Holy Ghost certifies more completely and helps us to feel deeply the truth of what we have come to know intellectually. Knowledge certified as true by the Holy Ghost yields understanding and produces an illumination, a comprehension, a perspective, and a depth of desire and commitment not obtainable through reason alone. As President Harold B. Lee frequently taught, "When we understand more than we know with our minds, when we understand with our hearts, then we know that the Spirit of the Lord is working upon us" ("When Your Heart Tells You Things Your Mind Does Not Know," 3).

In 1 Nephi 17 we find a classic example of the relationship between *knowledge* acquired through the mind and *understanding* obtained in the heart. Nephi has been commanded to build a ship, and in this chapter we learn about Laman and Lemuel's lack of faith and their opposition to and murmuring about that particular task. Nephi exhorts his brethren and highlights the importance of both reason and revelation.

"Ye are swift to do iniquity but slow to remember the Lord your God. Ye have seen an angel, and he spake unto you; yea, ye have heard his voice from time to time; and he hath spoken unto you in a still small voice, but ye were past feeling, that ye could not feel his words" (1 Nephi 17:45).

Certainly Laman and Lemuel had received knowledge about the purpose and importance of their journey in the wilderness, from loving parents, from Nephi, and from an angel of the Lord whom they had both seen and heard. But apparently they had not "applied [their] *hearts* to *understanding*" (Mosiah 12:27; emphasis added), they had not received confirming revelations, they did not feel the truthfulness of Nephi's words, and they were not blessed with understanding.

In our families and in our homes we are most receptive to learning, revelation, and the witnessing power of the Holy Ghost. Please pay particular attention to the following verses from section 68 of the Doctrine and Covenants, noting the use of the word *understand*.

"And again, inasmuch as parents have children in Zion, or in any of her stakes which are organized, that teach them not to *understand* the doctrine of repentance, faith in Christ the Son of the living God, and of baptism and the gift of the Holy Ghost by the laying on of the hands, when eight years old, the sin be upon the heads of the parents.

"For this shall be a law unto the inhabitants of Zion, or in any of her stakes which are organized" (Doctrine and Covenants 68:25–26, emphasis added).

These verses do not simply recommend or suggest that we teach our children. Rather, they outline a law unto the inhabitants of Zion—that we must teach our children *to understand*. Understanding is a spiritual outcome; it is a result. Simply engaging in the activity of teaching is not the responsibility we have been assigned. Rather, the charge is to teach children to understand.

Verses 25 and 26 in section 68 are an admonition for parents to create a home that is a house of learning wherein the Holy Ghost can reside and teach. In such a home the Holy Ghost brings conviction to the heart and teaches both children and parents to understand. Parents have important and vital roles to play as they

- create an appropriate spiritual environment and atmosphere in the home;
- invite the Spirit; and
- facilitate and assist the spiritual learning of children by explaining gospel truths, bearing pure testimony, asking and answering questions, and helping children to find answers to their questions and solutions to their challenges.

Ultimately, however, the parents cannot, in and of themselves, effect the kind of spiritual understanding described in the scriptures. The teacher is the Holy Ghost, and it is teaching by and the witness of the Spirit that produce understanding.

Parents and teachers need to do much more with children and young people than say, essentially, "Sit down and pay attention while we tell you what you need to know." Parents and leaders should become guides who help young people learn how to find answers for themselves. Youth need to act as agents and properly exercise their agency in order to obtain and retain strong testimonies and to become converted—instead of primarily depending spiritually upon someone else. We cannot borrow from another person what is necessary "to stand as witnesses of God at all times and in all things, and in all places" (Mosiah 18:9). With multitudes of secular influences trying to counteract the truth about and from God, no one can thrive by attempting to borrow light from the spiritual lamps of other people.

See video segment 4

The role of a teacher is to invite a learner to act in accordance with the truth taught by the Savior. A parent or teacher cannot push truth into the hearts of children and young people. Our best efforts can only bring the message of truth *unto* the heart (see 2 Nephi 33:1). Ultimately, a learner needs to exercise agency in righteousness and thereby invite the truth *into* the heart—and thereby seek to obtain the spiritual gift of understanding.

INTELLIGENCE

Intelligence is the righteous application of knowledge and understanding in action and judgment. It is the capstone that is constructed upon the cornerstone of knowledge and made stable by the keystone of understanding. Please notice in the following verses how understanding leads to righteous action.

"But a man of understanding walketh uprightly" (Proverbs 15:21).

"Give me understanding, and I shall keep thy law; yea, I shall observe it with my whole heart" (Psalm 119:34).

"Through thy precepts I get understanding: therefore I hate every false way" (Psalm 119:104).

"They had waxed strong in the knowledge of the truth; for they were men of a sound understanding and they had searched the scriptures diligently, that they might know the word of God. But this is not all; they had given themselves to much prayer, and fasting; therefore they had the spirit of prophecy, and the spirit of revelation, and when they taught, they taught with power and authority of God" (Alma 17:2–3).

Intelligence always is linked to righteousness. Recall in the New Testament the challenge to the sons of Sceva as they attempted to cast out evil spirits without proper authority:

"And the evil spirit answered and said, Jesus I know, and Paul I know; but who are ye?" (Acts 19:15).

Even the devils know. But they do not understand, and they certainly are not intelligent—because they "[know] not the mind of God" (Moses 4:6).

Please consider carefully the following verses from the Doctrine and Covenants.

"Whatever principle of intelligence we attain unto in this life, it will rise with us in the resurrection.

"And if a person gains more knowledge and intelligence in this life through his diligence and obedience than another, he will have so much the advantage in the world to come" (Doctrine and Covenants 130:18–19).

Please note the order in which *knowledge* and *intelligence* are listed in verse 19—with *knowledge* first and *intelligence* second. And also consider the parallel sequencing between *knowledge* and *intelligence* and the means by which they are acquired:

"And if a person gains more *knowledge* and *intelligence* in this life through his *diligence* and *obedience* . . ."

Interestingly, knowledge is associated with diligence. Significantly, intelligence is linked to obedience.

See video segment 7

Through persistent, effective, and diligent work, a person can accumulate knowledge in the form of facts, data, information, and experience. Intelligence, however, can only be gained through obedience. Thus, knowledge is a prerequisite to and foundation for true spiritual intelligence.

I next invite your attention to the sequence and pattern contained in verse 118 of section 88 of the Doctrine and Covenants.

"And as all have not faith, seek ye diligently and teach one another words of wisdom; yea, seek ye out of the best books words of wisdom; seek learning, even by study and also by faith" (Doctrine and Covenants 88:118).

The sequence in this verse complements what we learned in section 130. In fact, if we study these two revelations side by side we learn that knowledge is obtained through *diligent study* (*diligent* from verse 19 in section 130; *study* from verse 118 in section 88) and intelligence is gained through *faithful obedience.*

18 Whatever principle of *ᵃ*intelligence we attain unto in this life, it will rise with us in the *ᵇ*resurrection.
19 And if a person gains more *ᵃ*knowledge and intelligence in this life through his *ᵇ*diligence and obedience than another, he will have so much the *ᶜ*advantage in the world to come.

118 And as all have not *ᵃ*faith, seek ye diligently and *ᵇ*teach one another words of *ᶜ*wisdom; yea, seek ye out of the best *ᵈ*books words of wisdom; seek learning, even by study and also by faith.

The revelations teach us that "the glory of God is intelligence" (Doctrine and Covenants 93:36). We typically may think the word *intelligence* in this scripture denotes innate cognitive ability or a particular gift for academic or other types of work. In this verse, however, one of the meanings of *intelligence* is the application of the knowledge we obtain for righteous purposes. As President David O. McKay taught, the learning "for which the Church stands . . . is the application of knowledge to the development of a noble and Godlike character" ("True Education," 141).

See video segment 2

You and I are blessed in mortality with a multitude and variety of opportunities to learn and increase in intelligence—the intelligence defined as applying what we know for righteousness. Consequently, we should not equate intelligence with formal education, academic degrees, or worldly success. Some of the most educated people I have ever known had little or no intelligence. And some of the most intelligent people I have ever known had little or no formal education.

A pattern of knowledge related to doing, performing, and applying what we know for righteous purposes is found throughout the scriptures. As discussed in chapter 1, we are to use our moral agency to obtain and act in accordance with truth. We thus become agents who act rather than objects that are acted upon; we become "doers of the word, and not hearers only" (James 1:22).

"That every man may *act* in doctrine and principle pertaining to futurity, according to the moral agency which I have given unto him, that every man may be accountable for his own sins in the day of judgment" (Doctrine and Covenants 101:78; emphasis added).

Please note in this verse the phrase "act in doctrine." We might ordinarily think of doctrine as something we study, something we learn, and something we strive to remember. However, the Lord indicates in this revelation that doctrine is something you and I should *act in.* Ultimately, the Savior is interested not just in what we know but in spiritual intelligence—in how we apply what we know for righteous purposes.

"And this is the condemnation, that light is come into the world, and men loved darkness rather than light, because their deeds were evil.

"For every one that doeth evil hateth the light, neither cometh to the light, lest his deeds should be reproved.

"But he that *doeth truth* cometh to the light, that his deeds may be made manifest, that they are wrought in God" (John 3:19–21; emphasis added).

Would we characteristically consider truth to be something we do? Clearly, the message from the Lord in this revelation is that truth is something a person *doeth.* As King Benjamin instructed his people: "And now, if you believe . . . these things see that ye *do* them" (Mosiah 4:10; emphasis added).

And as the Savior taught the multitude gathered at the temple in the land of Bountiful:

"Now this is the commandment: Repent, all ye ends of the earth, and come unto me and be baptized in my name, that ye may be sanctified by the reception of the Holy Ghost, that ye may stand spotless before me at the last day.

"Verily, verily, I say unto you, this is my gospel; and ye know the things that ye must *do* in my church; for the works which ye have seen me *do* that shall ye also *do;* for that which ye have seen me *do* even that shall ye *do;*

"Therefore, if ye *do* these things blessed are ye, for ye shall be lifted up at the last day" (3 Nephi 27:20–22; emphasis added).

You and I may know the right things to do, but intelligence involves more than just knowing. If you and I are intelligent, we will consistently do the right things. Knowing that the gospel is true is important, good, and necessary. Intelligence is consistently being true to the gospel that we know.

Knowing that the principles of the gospel work in our lives is a good thing. However, intelligence is consistently working to apply the principles of the gospel in our lives.

We may know and understand that we should be active in the Church. Intelligence is living in such a way that the doctrines of the Church are active in us—an active and integral part of who we are, and what we are, and what we do, and what we think.

See video segment 13

Summary

In section 1 of the Doctrine and Covenants, the Savior describes this church as "the only true and living church upon the face of the . . . earth" (Doctrine and Covenants 1:30). Please consider the word *living* in that description. What is it that truly makes The Church of Jesus Christ of Latter-day Saints a living Church? It is a living Savior, the gift of the Holy Ghost and the attendant spiritual blessings and gifts, and the authority and power of the priesthood that make His Church both true and living. Appropriately seeking for knowledge, understanding, and intelligence is essential for each of us to become a living member of the Savior's living Church.

"For intelligence cleaveth unto intelligence; wisdom receiveth wisdom; truth embraceth truth; virtue loveth virtue; light cleaveth unto light" (Doctrine and Covenants 88:40).

Questions to Consider

1. What can and should I do to both *know* and *understand* the basic doctrines and principles of the restored gospel of Jesus Christ?

2. Because the "glory of God is intelligence," what can and should I do to increase in *intelligence?*

3. What can and should I do to become and remain a *living* member of the Savior's *living* Church?

Your Own Questions to Consider

1. _____

2. _____

3. _____

The video segments related to this chapter can be found at

desbook.com/learning

Related Readings
for Chapter Two

A pattern of knowledge and understanding leading to righteous action is evident throughout the scriptures.

Alma counseled his son Helaman, "O, remember, my son, and *learn wisdom* in thy youth; yea, learn in thy youth to *keep the commandments* of God" (Alma 37:35; emphasis added).

Paul declared in his second epistle to Timothy, "But *continue thou in the things which thou hast learned* and hast been assured of, knowing of whom thou hast learned them; And that from a child thou hast known the holy scriptures, which are able to make thee wise unto salvation through faith which is in Christ Jesus" (2 Timothy 3:14–15; emphasis added).

And the Savior admonished his latter-day disciples, "Wherefore, now let every man *learn his duty,* and to *act in the office* in which he is appointed, in all diligence" (Doctrine and Covenants 107:99; emphasis added).

The following readings focus upon the importance of *knowing* what we need to know, *living* as we know we should live, and *becoming* what the Master would have us become.

Ye Must Be Born Again

From *Ensign,* May 2007, 19–22

My boyhood home in California was located relatively close to large orchards of apricots, cherries, peaches, pears, and other delicious fruits. We also lived near fields of cucumbers, tomatoes, and a variety of vegetables.

As a boy I always looked forward to canning season. I did not like scrubbing the canning jars or working in our hot kitchen. But I did like working with my mom and dad. And I loved eating my work! I am sure I ate more fruit than ever made it into any of our canning jars.

My memories of time spent in the kitchen with Mom and Dad are stirred every time I see a bottle of home-canned cherries or peaches. The basic lessons I learned about temporal self-reliance and provident living while picking and canning produce have blessed me throughout my life. Interestingly, simple and ordinary experiences often provide the most important learning opportunities we ever have.

As an adult I have reflected upon the things I observed in our kitchen during canning season. I want to discuss some of the spiritual lessons we can learn from the process by which a cucumber becomes a pickle. I invite the Holy Ghost to be with us as we consider the significance of those lessons for me and for you as we come unto Christ and are spiritually reborn.

Cucumbers and Pickles

A pickle is a cucumber that has been transformed according to a specific recipe and series of steps. The first steps in the process of changing a cucumber into a pickle are *preparing* and *cleaning*. I remember many hours spent on the back porch of my home removing stems from and scrubbing dirt off of the cucumbers we had picked. My mom was very particular about the preparing and cleaning of the cucumbers. She had high standards of cleanliness and always inspected my work to make sure this important task was properly completed.

The next steps in this process of change are *immersing* and *saturating* the cucumbers in salt brine for an extended period of time. To prepare the brine, my mom always used a recipe she learned from her mother—a recipe with special ingredients and precise procedures. Cucumbers can only become pickles if they are totally and completely immersed in the brine for the prescribed time period. The curing process gradually alters the composition of the cucumber and produces the transparent appearance and distinctive taste of a pickle. An occasional sprinkle of or dip in the brine cannot produce the necessary transformation. Rather, steady, sustained, and complete immersion is required for the desired change to occur.

The final step in the process requires the *sealing* of the cured pickles in jars that have been sterilized and purified. The pickles are packed in canning jars, covered with boiling hot brine, and processed in a boiling-water-bath canner. All impurities must be removed from both the pickles and the bottles so the finished product can be protected and preserved. As this procedure is properly followed, the pickles can be stored and enjoyed for a long period of time.

To summarize, a cucumber becomes a pickle as it is prepared and cleaned, immersed in and saturated with salt brine, and sealed in a sterilized container. This procedure requires time and cannot be hurried, and none of the essential steps can be ignored or avoided.

A Mighty Change

The Lord's authorized servants repeatedly teach that one of the principal purposes of our mortal existence is to be spiritually changed and transformed through the Atonement of Jesus Christ. Alma declared:

"Marvel not that all mankind, yea, men and women, all nations, kindreds, tongues and people, must be born again; yea, born of God, changed from their carnal and fallen state, to a state of righteousness, being redeemed of God, becoming his sons and daughters;

"And thus they become new creatures; and unless they do this, they can in nowise inherit the kingdom of God" (Mosiah 27:25–26).

We are instructed to "come unto Christ, and be perfected in him, and deny [ourselves] of all ungodliness" (Moroni 10:32), to become "new creature[s]" in Christ (see 2 Corinthians 5:17), to put off "the natural man" (Mosiah 3:19), and to experience "a mighty change in us, or in our hearts, that we have no more disposition to do evil, but to do good continually" (Mosiah 5:2). Please note that the conversion described in these verses is mighty, not minor—a spiritual rebirth and fundamental change of what we feel and desire, what we think and do, and what we are. Indeed, the essence of the gospel of Jesus Christ entails a fundamental and permanent change in our very nature made possible through our reliance upon "the merits, and mercy, and grace of the Holy Messiah" (2 Nephi 2:8). As we choose to follow the Master, we choose to be changed—to be spiritually reborn.

Preparing and Cleaning

Just as a cucumber must be prepared and cleaned before it can be changed into a pickle, so you and I can be prepared with "the words of faith and of good doctrine" (1 Timothy 4:6) and initially cleansed through the ordinances and covenants administered by the authority of the Aaronic Priesthood.

"And the lesser priesthood continued, which priesthood holdeth the key of the ministering of angels and the preparatory gospel;

"Which gospel is the gospel of repentance and of baptism, and the remission of sins" (Doctrine and Covenants 84:26–27).

And the Lord has established a high standard of cleanliness.

"Wherefore teach it unto your children, that all men, everywhere, must repent, or they can in nowise inherit the kingdom of God, for no unclean thing can dwell there, or dwell in his presence" (Moses 6:57).

Proper preparing and cleaning are the first basic steps in the process of being born again.

Immersing and Saturating

Just as a cucumber is transformed into a pickle as it is immersed in and saturated with salt brine, so you and I are born again as we are absorbed by and in the gospel of Jesus Christ. As we honor and "observe the covenants" (Doctrine and Covenants 42:13) into which we have entered, as we "feast upon the words of Christ" (2 Nephi 32:3), as we "pray unto the Father with all the energy of heart" (Moroni 7:48), and as we "serve [God] with all [of our] heart, might, mind and strength" (Doctrine and Covenants 4:2), then:

"Because of the covenant which ye have made ye shall be called the children of Christ, his sons, and his daughters; for behold, this day he hath spiritually begotten you; for ye say that your hearts are changed through faith on his name; therefore, ye are born of him and have become his sons and his daughters" (Mosiah 5:7).

The spiritual rebirth described in this verse typically does not occur quickly or all at once; it is an ongoing process—not a single event. Line upon line and precept upon precept, gradually and almost imperceptibly, our motives, our thoughts, our words, and our deeds become aligned with the will of God. This phase of the transformation process requires time, persistence, and patience.

A cucumber only becomes a pickle through steady, sustained, and complete immersion in salt brine. Significantly, salt is the key ingredient in the recipe. Salt frequently is used in the scriptures as a symbol both of a covenant and of a covenant people. And just as salt is essential in transforming a cucumber into a pickle, so covenants are central to our spiritual rebirth.

We begin the process of being born again through exercising faith in Christ, repenting of our sins, and being baptized by immersion for the remission of sins by one having priesthood authority.

"Therefore we are buried with him by baptism into death: that like as Christ was raised up from the dead by the glory of the Father, even so we also should walk in newness of life" (Romans 6:4).

And after we come out of the waters of baptism, our souls need to be continuously immersed in and saturated with the truth and the light of the Savior's gospel. Sporadic and shallow dipping in the doctrine of Christ and partial participation in His restored Church cannot produce the spiritual transformation that enables us to walk in a newness of life. Rather, fidelity to covenants, constancy of commitment, and offering our whole soul unto God are required if we are to receive the blessings of eternity.

"I would that ye should come unto Christ, who is the Holy One of Israel, and partake of his salvation, and the power of his redemption. Yea, come unto him, and offer your whole souls as an offering unto him, and continue in fasting and praying, and endure to the end; and as the Lord liveth ye will be saved" (Omni 1:26).

Total immersion in and saturation with the Savior's gospel are essential steps in the process of being born again.

Purifying and Sealing

Cured cucumbers are packed into sterilized jars and heat processed in order to remove impurities and to seal the containers from external contaminants. The boiling-water-bath procedure enables the pickles to be both protected and preserved over a long period of time. In a similar way, we progressively become purified and sanctified as you and I are washed in the blood of the Lamb, are born again, and receive the ordinances and honor the covenants that are administered by the authority of the Melchizedek Priesthood.

"Nevertheless they did fast and pray oft, and did wax stronger and stronger in their humility, and firmer and firmer in the faith of Christ, unto the filling their souls with joy and consolation, yea, even to the purifying and the sanctification of their hearts, which sanctification cometh because of their yielding their hearts unto God" (Helaman 3:35).

The word *sealing* does not refer exclusively to the ordinance of eternal marriage performed in the house of the Lord. Rather, I am using this particular word as explained in the 76th section of the Doctrine and Covenants:

"This is the testimony of the gospel of Christ concerning them who shall come forth in the resurrection of the just—

"They are they who received the testimony of Jesus, and believed on his name and were baptized after the manner of his burial, being buried in the water in his name, and this according to the commandment which he has given—

"That by keeping the commandments they might be washed and cleansed from all their sins, and receive the Holy Spirit by the laying on of the hands of him who is ordained and sealed unto this power;

"And who overcome by faith, and are sealed by the Holy Spirit of promise, which the Father sheds forth upon all those who are just and true" (vv. 50–53).

The Holy Spirit of Promise is the ratifying power of the Holy Ghost. When sealed by the Holy Spirit of Promise, an ordinance, vow, or covenant is binding on earth and in heaven (see Doctrine and Covenants 132:7). Receiving this "stamp of approval" from the Holy Ghost is the result of faithfulness, integrity, and steadfastness in honoring gospel covenants "in [the] process of time" (Moses 7:21). However, this sealing can be forfeited through unrighteousness and transgression.

Purifying and sealing by the Holy Spirit of Promise constitute the culminating steps in the process of being born again.

"In the Energy of My Soul"

My beloved brothers and sisters, I pray this parable of the pickle may help us to evaluate our lives and to better understand the eternal importance of spiritual rebirth. With Alma, "I speak in the energy of my soul" (Alma 5:43).

"I say unto you that this is the order after which I am called, yea, to preach unto my beloved brethren, yea, and every one that dwelleth in the land; yea, to preach unto all, both old and young, both bond and free; yea, I say unto you the aged, and also the middle aged, and the rising generation; yea, to cry unto them that they must repent and be born again" (Alma 5:49).

I witness the reality and divinity of a living Savior who invites us to come unto Him and be transformed. I testify His Church and priesthood authority have been restored through the Prophet Joseph Smith. Through faith in Christ, we can be spiritually prepared and cleansed from sin, immersed in and saturated with His gospel, and purified and sealed by the Holy Spirit of Promise—even born again.

Clean Hands and a Pure Heart

From *Ensign,* November 2007, 80–83

I have fond childhood memories of my mother reading Book of Mormon stories to me. She had a way of making the scriptural episodes come alive in my youthful imagination, and I did not doubt that my mother had a witness of the truthfulness of that sacred record. I especially remember her description of the Savior's visit to the American continent following His Resurrection and of His teachings to the people in the land of Bountiful. Through the simple consistency of her example and testimony, my mother kindled in me the first flames of faith in the Savior and in His latter-day Church. I came to know for myself that the Book of Mormon is another testament of Jesus Christ and contains the fulness of His everlasting gospel (see Doctrine and Covenants 27:5).

I want to review with you one of my favorite Book of Mormon events, the Savior's appearance in the New World, and discuss His instruction to the multitude about the sanctifying power of the Holy Ghost.

The Savior's Ministry in the New World

During the Lord's three-day ministry in the New World, He taught His doctrine, authorized His disciples to perform priesthood ordinances, healed the sick, prayed for the people, and lovingly blessed the children. As the Savior's time with the people was drawing to a close, He succinctly summarized the fundamental principles of His gospel.

Said He, "Now this is the commandment: Repent, all ye ends of the earth, and come unto me and be baptized in my name, that ye may be sanctified by the reception of the Holy Ghost, that ye may stand spotless before me at the last day" (3 Nephi 27:20).

The basic principles outlined by the Master in this scripture are essential for us to understand and apply in our lives. First was repentance, "a turning of the heart and will to God, and a renunciation of sin" (Bible Dictionary, "Repentance," 760). As we appropriately seek for and receive the spiritual gift of faith in the Redeemer, we then turn to and rely upon the merits, the mercy, and the grace of the Holy Messiah (see 2 Nephi 2:8). Repentance is the sweet fruit that comes from faith in the Savior and involves turning toward God and away from sin.

The risen Lord next explained the importance of coming unto Him. The multitude of people gathered together at the temple were invited literally to come forth unto the Savior "one by one" (3 Nephi 11:15) to feel the prints of the nails in the Master's hands and feet and to thrust their hands into His side. Each individual who had this experience "did know of a surety and did bear record, that it was he" (v. 15), even Jesus Christ, who had come.

The Savior also taught the people to come unto Him through sacred covenants, and He reminded them that they were "the children of the covenant" (3 Nephi 20:26). He emphasized the eternal importance of the ordinances of baptism (see 3 Nephi 11:19–39) and of receiving the Holy Ghost (see 3 Nephi 11:35–36; 12:6; 18:36–38). In a similar manner, you and I are admonished to turn toward and learn from Christ and to come unto Him through the covenants and ordinances of His restored gospel. As we do so, we will eventually and ultimately come to know Him (see John 17:3), "in his own time, and in his own way, and according to his own will" (Doctrine and Covenants 88:68), as did the people in the land of Bountiful.

Repenting and coming unto Christ through the covenants and ordinances of salvation are prerequisite to and a preparation for being sanctified by the reception of the Holy Ghost and standing spotless before God at the last day. I now want to focus our attention upon the sanctifying influence the Holy Ghost can be in our lives.

Our Spiritual Journey

The gate of baptism leads to the strait and narrow path and to the destination of putting off the natural man and becoming a saint through the Atonement of Christ the Lord (see Mosiah 3:19). The purpose of our mortal journey is not merely to see the sights on earth or to expend our allotment of time on self-centered pursuits; rather, we are to "walk in newness of life" (Romans 6:4), to become sanctified by yielding our hearts unto God (see Helaman 3:35), and to obtain "the mind of Christ" (1 Corinthians 2:16).

We are commanded and instructed to so live that our fallen nature is changed through the sanctifying power of the Holy Ghost. President Marion G. Romney taught that the baptism of fire by the Holy Ghost "converts [us] from carnality to spirituality. It cleanses, heals, and purifies the soul. . . . Faith in the Lord Jesus Christ, repentance, and water baptism are all preliminary and prerequisite to it, but [the baptism of fire] is the consummation. To receive [this baptism of fire] is to have one's garments washed in the atoning blood of Jesus Christ" (*Learning for the Eternities,* 133; see also 3 Nephi 27:19–20).

Hence, as we are born again and strive to always have His

Spirit to be with us, the Holy Ghost sanctifies and refines our souls as if by fire (see 2 Nephi 31:13–14, 17). Ultimately, we are to stand spotless before God.

The gospel of Jesus Christ encompasses much more than avoiding, overcoming, and being cleansed from sin and the bad influences in our lives; it also essentially entails doing good, being good, and becoming better. Repenting of our sins and seeking forgiveness are spiritually necessary, and we must always do so. But remission of sin is not the only or even the ultimate purpose of the gospel. To have our hearts changed by the Holy Spirit such that "we have no more disposition to do evil, but to do good continually" (Mosiah 5:2), as did King Benjamin's people, is the covenant responsibility we have accepted. This mighty change is not simply the result of working harder or developing greater individual discipline. Rather, it is the consequence of a fundamental change in our desires, our motives, and our natures made possible through the Atonement of Christ the Lord. Our spiritual purpose is to overcome both sin and the desire to sin, both the taint and the tyranny of sin.

Prophets throughout the ages have emphasized the dual requirements of (1) avoiding and overcoming bad and (2) doing good and becoming better. Consider the penetrating questions posed by the Psalmist:

"Who shall ascend into the hill of the Lord? or who shall stand in his holy place?

"He that hath clean hands, and a pure heart; who hath not lifted up his soul unto vanity, nor sworn deceitfully" (Psalm 24:3–4).

It is possible for us to have clean hands but not have a pure heart. Please notice that both clean hands and a pure heart are required to ascend into the hill of the Lord and to stand in His holy place.

Let me suggest that hands are made clean through the process of putting off the natural man and by overcoming sin and the evil influences in our lives through the Savior's Atonement. Hearts are purified as we receive His strengthening power to do good and become better. All of our worthy desires and good works, as necessary as they are, can never produce clean hands and a pure heart. It is the Atonement of Jesus Christ that provides both a *cleansing and redeeming power* that helps us to overcome sin and a *sanctifying and strengthening power* that helps us to become better than we ever could by relying only upon our own strength. The infinite Atonement is for both the sinner and for the saint in each of us.

In the Book of Mormon, we find the masterful teachings of King Benjamin concerning the mission and Atonement of Jesus Christ. The simple doctrine he taught caused the congregation to fall to the earth, for the fear of the Lord had come upon them. "And they had viewed themselves in their own carnal state, even less than the dust of the earth. And they all cried aloud with one voice, saying: O have mercy, and apply the atoning blood of Christ that we may receive *forgiveness of our sins,* and our *hearts may be purified;* for we believe in Jesus Christ, the Son of God, who created heaven and earth, and all things; who shall come down among the children of men" (Mosiah 4:2; emphasis added).

Again in this verse we find the twofold blessing of both forgiveness of sin, suggesting clean hands, and the transformation of our nature, signifying pure hearts.

As King Benjamin concluded his instruction, he reiterated the importance of these two basic aspects of spiritual development.

"And now, for the sake of these things which I have spoken unto you—that is, for the sake of *retaining a remission of your sins from day to day,* that *ye may walk guiltless before God*—I would that ye should impart of your substance to the poor" (Mosiah 4:26; emphasis added).

Our sincere desire should be to have both clean hands *and* a pure heart—both a remission of sins from day to day *and* to walk guiltless before God. Clean hands alone will not be enough when we stand before Him who is pure and who, as "a lamb without blemish and without spot" (1 Peter 1:19), freely spilled His precious blood for us.

Line upon Line

Some may think the spiritual progress I am describing is not attainable in their lives. We may believe these truths apply to others but not to us.

We will not attain a state of perfection in this life, but we can and should press forward with faith in Christ along the strait and narrow path and make steady progress toward our eternal destiny. The Lord's pattern for spiritual development is "line upon line, precept upon precept, here a little and there a little" (2 Nephi 28:30). Small, steady, incremental spiritual improvements are the steps the Lord would have us take. Preparing to walk guiltless before God is one of the primary purposes of mortality and the pursuit of a lifetime; it does not result from sporadic spurts of intense spiritual activity.

I witness that the Savior will strengthen and assist us to make sustained, paced progress. The example in the Book of Mormon of "many, exceedingly great many" (Alma 13:12) in the ancient Church who were pure and spotless before God is a source of encouragement and comfort to me. I suspect those members of the ancient Church were ordinary men and women just like you and me. These individuals could not look upon sin save it were with abhorrence, and they "were made pure and entered into the rest of the Lord their God" (v. 12). And these principles and this process of spiritual progress apply to each of us equally and always.

Moroni's Concluding Invitation

The requirement to put off the natural man and become a saint, to avoid and overcome bad and to do and become good, to have clean hands and a pure heart, is a recurring theme throughout the Book of Mormon. In fact, Moroni's concluding invitation at the end of the book is a summary of this theme.

"Yea, come unto Christ, and be perfected in him, and deny yourselves of all ungodliness; and if ye shall deny yourselves of all ungodliness, and love God with all your might, mind and strength, then is his grace sufficient for you, that by his grace ye may be perfect in Christ. . . .

"And again, if ye by the grace of God are perfect in Christ, and deny not his power, then are ye sanctified in Christ by the grace of God, through the shedding of the blood of Christ, which is in the covenant of the Father unto the *remission of your sins,* that *ye become holy, without spot*" (Moroni 10:32–33; emphasis added).

May you and I repent with sincerity of heart and truly come unto Christ. I pray that we will seek through the Savior's Atonement to have both clean hands and a pure heart, that we may become holy, without spot. I witness that Jesus Christ is the Son of the Eternal Father and our Savior. He who is without spot redeems us from sin and strengthens us to do good and to become better.

Watching with All Perseverance

From *Ensign,* May 2010, 40–43

Recently I was driving my car as drops of rain from a thunderstorm began to fall on the windshield. On the side of the road, an electronic sign displayed a timely warning: "Standing Water Ahead." The surface on which I was driving appeared to be quite safe. But this vital information enabled me to prepare for a potential hazard I had not expected and could not yet see. As I continued toward my destination, I slowed down and watched carefully for additional signs of danger.

Early warning signals are evident in many aspects of our lives. For example, a fever can be a first symptom of sickness or disease. Various financial and labor market indicators are used to forecast future trends in local and national economies. And depending upon the area of the world in which we live, we may receive flood, avalanche, hurricane, tsunami, tornado, or winter storm warnings.

We also are blessed by spiritual early warning signals as a source of protection and direction in our lives. Recall how Noah was alerted by God of things not yet seen, and he "prepared [the] ark to the saving of his house" (Hebrews 11:7).

Lehi was warned to leave Jerusalem and take his family into the wilderness because the people to whom he had declared repentance sought to kill him (see 1 Nephi 2:1–2).

The Savior Himself was spared through an angelic warning: "Behold, the angel of the Lord appeareth to Joseph in a dream, saying, Arise, and take the young child and his mother, and flee into Egypt, and be thou there until I bring thee word: for Herod will seek the young child to destroy him" (Matthew 2:13).

Consider the language of the Lord in the revelation known as the Word of Wisdom: "In consequence of evils and designs which do and will exist in the hearts of conspiring men in the last days, I have warned you, and forewarn you, by giving unto you this word of wisdom by revelation" (Doctrine and Covenants 89:4).

Spiritual warnings should lead to increasingly vigilant watching. You and I live in "a day of warning" (Doctrine and Covenants 63:58). And because we have been and will be warned, we need to be, as the Apostle Paul admonished, "watching . . . with all perseverance" (Ephesians 6:18).

There is a spiritual early warning system that can help parents in Zion to be watchful and discerning concerning their children. This early warning system applies to children of all ages and contains three basic components: (1) reading and talking about the Book of Mormon with your children, (2) bearing testimony of gospel truths spontaneously with your children, and (3) inviting children as gospel learners to act and not merely be acted upon. Parents who do these things faithfully will be blessed to recognize early signals of spiritual growth in or challenges with their children and be better prepared to receive inspiration to strengthen and help those children.

Component Number One:
Reading and Talking about the Book of Mormon

The Book of Mormon contains the fulness of the Savior's gospel and is the only book the Lord Himself has testified to be true (see Doctrine and Covenants 17:6; see also Russell M. Nelson, "A

Testimony of the Book of Mormon," 70). Indeed, the Book of Mormon is the keystone of our religion.

The convincing and converting powers of the Book of Mormon come from both a central focus upon the Lord Jesus Christ and the inspired plainness and clarity of its teachings. Nephi declared, "My soul delighteth in plainness unto my people, that they may learn" (2 Nephi 25:4). The root word *plain* in this verse does not refer to things that are ordinary or simple; rather, it denotes instruction that is clear and easily understood.

The Book of Mormon is the most correct of any book on earth because it centers upon the Truth (see John 14:6; 1 Nephi 13:40), even Jesus Christ, and restores the plain and precious things that have been taken away from the true gospel (see 1 Nephi 13:26, 28–29, 32, 34–35, 40). The unique combination of these two factors—a focus on the Savior and the plainness of the teachings—powerfully invites the confirming witness of the third member of the Godhead, even the Holy Ghost. Consequently, the Book of Mormon speaks to the spirit and to the heart of the reader like no other volume of scripture.

The Prophet Joseph Smith taught that abiding by the precepts found in the Book of Mormon would help us "get nearer to God" than any other book (*Teachings: Joseph Smith,* 64). Regular reading of and talking about the Book of Mormon invite the power to resist temptation and to produce feelings of love within our families. And discussions about the doctrines and principles in the Book of Mormon provide opportunities for parents to observe their children, to listen to them, to learn from them, and to teach them.

Youth of all ages, even infants, can and do respond to the distinctive spirit of the Book of Mormon. Children may not understand all of the words and stories, but they certainly can feel the "familiar spirit" described by Isaiah (Isaiah 29:4; see also 2 Nephi

26:16). And the questions a child asks, the observations a child shares, and the discussions that occur provide crucial spiritual early warning signals. Importantly, such conversations can help parents to discern what their children are learning, thinking, and feeling about the truths contained in this sacred volume of scripture, as well as the difficulties they may be facing.

Component Number Two: Bearing Testimony Spontaneously

Testimony is personal knowledge, based upon the witness of the Holy Ghost, that certain facts of eternal significance are true. The Holy Ghost is the messenger for the Father and the Son and the teacher of and guide to all truth (see John 14:26; 16:13). Thus, "by the power of the Holy Ghost [we] may know the truth of all things" (Moroni 10:5).

The knowledge and spiritual conviction we receive from the Holy Ghost are the result of revelation. Seeking for and obtaining these blessings require a sincere heart, real intent, and faith in Christ (see Moroni 10:4). A personal testimony also brings responsibility and accountability.

Parents should be vigilant and spiritually attentive to spontaneously occurring opportunities to bear testimony to their children. Such occasions need not be programmed, scheduled, or scripted. In fact, the less regimented such testimony sharing is, the greater the likelihood for edification and lasting impact. "Neither take ye thought beforehand what ye shall say; but treasure up in your minds continually the words of life, and it shall be given you in the very hour that portion that shall be meted unto every man" (Doctrine and Covenants 84:85).

For example, a naturally occurring family conversation at dinner may be the perfect setting for a parent to recount and testify of specific blessings he or she received during the course of relatively routine activities that day. And a testimony need not always begin with the phrase "I bear you my testimony." Our witness can be declared as simply as "I know I was blessed with inspiration at work today" or "The truth in this scripture always has been a powerful source of direction for me." Similar opportunities to bear testimony also can arise while traveling together in a car or bus or in a multitude of other settings.

The reactions of children to such impromptu testimony bearing and their eagerness or reluctance to participate are potent sources of spiritual early warning signals. A child's expression about a lesson learned in family scripture study or a candid statement of concern about a gospel principle or practice can be most illuminating and help parents better understand a child's specific question or needs. Such discussions—especially when parents are as eager to listen intently as they are to talk—can foster a supportive and secure environment in the home and encourage ongoing communication about difficult topics.

Component Number Three: Inviting Children to Act

In the grand division of all of God's creations, there are "things to act and things to be acted upon" (2 Nephi 2:14). As children of our Heavenly Father, we have been blessed with the gift of moral agency, the capacity and power of independent action. Endowed with agency, we are agents, and we primarily are to act and not merely be acted upon—especially as we "seek learning . . . by study and also by faith" (Doctrine and Covenants 88:118).

As gospel learners, we should be "doers of the word, and not hearers only" (James 1:22). Our hearts are opened to the influence of the Holy Ghost as we properly exercise agency and act in accordance with correct principles—and we thereby invite His teaching and testifying power. Parents have the sacred responsibility to help children to act and to seek learning by faith. And a child is never too young to take part in this pattern of learning.

Giving a man a fish feeds him for one meal. Teaching a man to fish feeds him for a lifetime. As parents and gospel instructors, you and I are not in the business of distributing fish; rather, our work is to help our children learn "to fish" and to become spiritually steadfast. This vital objective is best accomplished as we encourage our children to act in accordance with correct principles—as we help them to learn by doing. "If any man will do his will, he shall know of the doctrine, whether it be of God" (John 7:17). Such learning requires spiritual, mental, and physical exertion and not just passive reception.

Inviting children as gospel learners to act and not merely be acted upon builds on reading and talking about the Book of Mormon and bearing testimony spontaneously in the home. Imagine, for example, a family home evening in which children are invited and expected to come prepared to ask questions about what they are reading and learning in the Book of Mormon—or about an issue that recently was emphasized in a gospel discussion or spontaneous testimony in the home. And imagine further that the children ask questions the parents are not prepared adequately to answer. Some parents might be apprehensive about such an unstructured approach to home evening. But the best family home evenings are not necessarily the product of preprepared, purchased, or downloaded packets of outlines and visual aids. What a glorious opportunity for family members to search the scriptures together and to be tutored by the Holy Ghost. "For the preacher was no better than the hearer, neither was the teacher any better than the learner; . . . and they did all labor, every man according to his strength" (Alma 1:26).

Are you and I helping our children become agents who act and seek learning by study and by faith, or have we trained our children to wait to be taught and acted upon? Are we as parents primarily giving our children the equivalent of spiritual fish to eat, or are we consistently helping them to act, to learn for themselves, and to stand steadfast and immovable? Are we helping our children become anxiously engaged in asking, seeking, and knocking? (see 3 Nephi 14:7).

The spiritual understanding you and I have been blessed to receive, and which has been confirmed as true in our hearts, simply cannot be given to our children. The tuition of diligence and of learning by study and also by faith must be paid to obtain and personally "own" such knowledge. Only in this way can what is known in the mind also be felt in the heart. Only in this way can a child move beyond relying upon the spiritual knowledge and experiences of parents and adults and claim those blessings for himself or herself. Only in this way can our children be prepared spiritually for the challenges of mortality.

Promise and Testimony

I bear witness that parents who consistently read and talk about the Book of Mormon with their children, who share testimony spontaneously with their children, and who invite children as gospel learners to act and not merely be acted upon will be blessed with eyes that can see afar off (see Moses 6:27) and with ears that can hear the sound of the trumpet (see Ezekiel 33:2–16). The spiritual discernment and inspiration you will receive from the combination of these three holy habits will enable you to stand as watchmen on the tower for your families—"watching . . . with all perseverance" (Ephesians 6:18)—to the blessing of your immediate family and your future posterity.

CHAPTER THREE

PRAYERFUL INQUIRY:
ASKING, SEEKING, AND KNOCKING

Nephi provides a powerful example of a basic principle that is essential to our spiritual learning and progress as individuals and as families, to our work of the ministry, and to the growth of the latter-day kingdom of God on the earth.

After being carried away in the spirit and seeing all the things his father, Lehi, had seen in the vision of the tree of life, Nephi returned to the tent of his father.

"And it came to pass that I beheld my brethren, and they were disputing one with another concerning the things which my father had spoken unto them.

"For he truly spake many great things unto them, which were *hard to be understood, save a man should inquire of the Lord;* and they being hard in their hearts, therefore they did not look unto the Lord as they ought" (1 Nephi 15:2–3; emphasis added).

Nephi was grieved because of the hardness of the hearts of his brethren, and he counseled with them to learn the cause of their disputations.

"And they said: Behold, we cannot understand the words

which our father hath spoken concerning the natural branches of the olive-tree, and also concerning the Gentiles" (1 Nephi 15:7).

In a penetrating question, Nephi next identified a basic principle of spiritual learning.

"And I said unto them: Have ye *inquired of the Lord?*" (1 Nephi 15:8; emphasis added).

Nephi then described an important pattern associated with learning the things of God.

"Do ye not remember the things which the Lord hath said?—If ye will not harden your hearts, and ask me in faith, believing that ye shall receive, with diligence in keeping my commandments, surely these things shall be made known unto you" (1 Nephi 15:11).

See video segment 8

Inquire is an action word that denotes asking, requesting, petitioning, soliciting, investigating, and exploring. Inquiring of the Lord requires from us much more than merely or routinely asking; it is a spiritually demanding and rigorous process. Sincere desire, diligent preparation, and faithful confidence in and commitment to act upon the expected instruction precede prayerful inquiry. Thus, inquiring of the Lord includes asking, but asking alone is not all that is involved in inquiring.

Oliver Cowdery learned this important lesson in 1829 as he was assisting Joseph Smith in the translation of the Book of Mormon.

"Behold, you have not understood; you have supposed that I would give it unto you, when you took no thought save it was to ask me.

"But, behold, I say unto you, that you must study it out in your mind; then you must ask me if it be right, and if it is right I will cause that your bosom shall burn within you; therefore, you shall feel that it is right" (Doctrine and Covenants 9:7–8).

The scriptures are replete with examples of inquiring of the Lord.

"And it came to pass that I, Nephi, did make out of wood a bow, and out of a straight stick, an arrow; wherefore, I did arm myself with a bow and an arrow, with a sling and with stones. And I said unto my father: Whither shall I go to obtain food?

"And it came to pass that he did *inquire* of the Lord. . . .

"And it came to pass that the voice of the Lord came unto my father" (1 Nephi 16:23–25; emphasis added).

"Wherefore, I must tell you the truth according to the plainness of the word of God. For behold, as I *inquired* of the Lord, thus came the word unto me, saying: Jacob, get thou up into the temple on the morrow, and declare the word which I shall give thee unto this people" (Jacob 2:11; emphasis added).

"And now the spirit of Alma was again troubled; and he went and *inquired* of the Lord what he should do concerning this matter, for he feared that he should do wrong in the sight of God" (Mosiah 26:13; emphasis added).

"And king Mosiah went and *inquired* of the Lord if he should let his sons go up among the Lamanites to preach the word" (Mosiah 28:6; emphasis added).

"But the king said unto them: Behold, the Nephites will destroy us, because of the many murders and sins we have committed against them.

"And Ammon said: I will go and *inquire* of the Lord, and if he say unto us, go down unto our brethren, will ye go?

"And the king said unto him: Yea, if the Lord saith unto us go, we will go down unto our brethren" (Alma 27:6–8; emphasis added).

"Therefore, there is a time appointed unto men that they shall rise from the dead; and there is a space between the time of death and the resurrection. And now, concerning this space of time, what becometh of the souls of men is the thing which I have *inquired* diligently of the Lord to know; and this is the thing of which I do know" (Alma 40:9; emphasis added).

"And it came to pass that Jared spake again unto his brother, saying: Go and *inquire* of the Lord whether he will drive us out of the land, and if he will drive us out of the land, cry unto him whither we shall go. And who knoweth but the Lord will carry us forth into a land which is choice above all the earth? And if it so be, let us be faithful unto the Lord, that we may receive it for our inheritance" (Ether 1:38; emphasis added).

"For immediately after I had learned these things of you I *inquired* of the Lord concerning the matter. And the word of the Lord came to me by the power of the Holy Ghost" (Moroni 8:7; emphasis added).

"We still continued the work of translation, when, in the ensuing month (May, 1829), we on a certain day went into the woods to pray and *inquire* of the Lord respecting baptism for the remission of sins, that we found mentioned in the translation of the plates" (Joseph Smith—History 1:68; emphasis added).

"Now, as you have *asked*, behold, I say unto you . . .

"And if thou wilt *inquire*, thou shalt know mysteries which are great and marvelous; therefore thou shalt exercise thy gift, that thou mayest find out mysteries, that thou mayest bring many to the knowledge of the truth, yea, convince them of the error of their ways. . . .

"Verily, verily, I say unto thee, blessed art thou for what thou hast done; for thou hast *inquired* of me, and behold, as often as thou hast *inquired* thou hast received instruction of my Spirit" (Doctrine and Covenants 6:6, 11, 14; emphasis added).

"In case of difficulty respecting doctrine or principle, if there is not a sufficiency written to make the case clear to the minds of the council, the president may *inquire* and obtain the mind of the Lord by revelation" (Doctrine and Covenants 102:23; emphasis added).

"And again Moses said: I will not cease to call upon God, I have other things to *inquire* of him: for his glory has been upon me" (Moses 1:18; emphasis added).

Prayerful inquiry is a necessary prerequisite to inspiration and revelation. This pattern is evident in the previously mentioned experiences of Nephi, Jacob, Alma, King Mosiah, Ammon, the brother of Jared, Mormon, Joseph Smith, Oliver Cowdery, and Moses, and in relation to nearly all of the revelations that have been received in this dispensation.

Ask, Seek, Knock

Three components of prayerful inquiry are emphasized repeatedly in the scriptures: asking, seeking, and knocking.

"*Ask,* and it shall be given you; *seek,* and ye shall find; *knock,* and it shall be opened unto you" (Matthew 7:7; emphasis added).

"And I say unto you, *Ask,* and it shall be given you; *seek,* and ye shall find; *knock,* and it shall be opened unto you" (Luke 11:9; emphasis added).

"Wherefore, now after I have spoken these words, if ye cannot understand them it will be because ye *ask* not, neither do ye *knock;* wherefore, ye are not brought into the light, but must perish in the dark" (2 Nephi 32:4; emphasis added).

"*Ask,* and it shall be given unto you; *seek,* and ye shall find; *knock,* and it shall be opened unto you" (3 Nephi 14:7; emphasis added).

"Draw near unto me and I will draw near unto you; seek me diligently and ye shall find me; *ask,* and ye shall receive; *knock,* and it shall be opened unto you (Doctrine and Covenants 88:63; emphasis added).

See video segment 9

Asking, seeking, and knocking are active components of prayerful inquiry and denote initiating, engaging anxiously, pressing forward steadfastly, and acting. These three interrelated and overlapping elements of inquiring are vital elements in the pattern the Lord has employed when giving direction, instruction, and revelation. Honesty, effort, commitment, and persistence are required in asking, seeking, and knocking.

One of the most well-known episodes in the life of Joseph Smith was his reading of verses about prayer and faith in the New Testament. As young Joseph was seeking to know the truth about religion, he read the following verses in the first chapter of James:

"If any of you lack wisdom, let him ask of God, that giveth to all men liberally, and upbraideth not; and it shall be given him.

"But let him ask in faith, nothing wavering" (James 1:5–6).

Please note the requirement to ask in faith—which I understand to mean the necessity not only to express but to do, the dual obligation both to plead and to perform, the requirement to communicate and to act.

Pondering this biblical text inspired Joseph to retire to a grove of trees near his home to inquire of the Lord and to seek for spiritual knowledge. Consider the action-oriented questions Joseph had formulated in his mind and felt in his heart—and which he took into the grove.

"In the midst of this war of words and tumult of opinions, I often said to myself: What is to be done? Who of all these parties are right; or, are they all wrong together? If any one of them be right, which is it, and how shall I know it? . . .

"My object in going to inquire of the Lord was to know which of all the sects was right, that I might know which to join. No sooner, therefore, did I get possession of myself, so as to be able to speak, than I asked the Personages who stood above me in the light, which of all the sects was right . . . and which I should join" (Joseph Smith—History 1:10, 18).

Notice that Joseph's questions focused not just on what he needed to know but also on what he needed to do. And his very first question centered on what was to be *done!* His prayerful inquiry was not simply: Which church is right? His question was: Which church should he join? Thus, the dispensation of the fulness of times commenced because young Joseph Smith inquired of the Lord in faith through asking, seeking, and knocking.

Three years following the First Vision, Moroni appeared to Joseph in response to the young prophet's earnest prayer to know his standing before the Lord. In Joseph Smith's history we learn about the concerns in young Joseph's heart that preceded the visitation of Moroni.

"After I had retired to my bed for the night, I betook myself to prayer and supplication to Almighty God for forgiveness of all my sins and follies, and also for a manifestation to me, that I might know of my state and standing before him" (Joseph Smith—History 1:29).

Again, please note that Joseph had a specific question about his standing before the Lord, and Joseph knelt in prayer to ask, to seek, and to knock.

Nearly all of the early revelations to individuals in the Church—to Joseph Smith Sr.; Hyrum Smith; Oliver Cowdery; Joseph Knight; David, Peter, John, and Christian Whitmer—were given in answer to the inquiry of these men to know their duty with respect to the work of the Lord then rolling forth. Each of these men came to the Prophet Joseph with a particular question or questions. They were following the Lord's direction: "And if ye are purified and cleansed from all sin, ye shall ask whatsoever you will in the name of Jesus and it shall be done. But know this, it shall be given you what you shall ask" (Doctrine and Covenants 50:29–30). These brethren were anxiously engaged in the process of inquiring of the Lord through asking, seeking, and knocking.

Consider two additional examples of prayerful inquiry from the early days of the Restoration.

Inspired direction on Church organization and government (Doctrine and Covenants 20) was given in response to Joseph's and Oliver's prayers and questions concerning priesthood and organizational issues.

The great revelation on priesthood and the relationships of the quorums to each other (Doctrine and Covenants 107) was also given in response to a petition by the Twelve to the Prophet Joseph Smith.

"Hearken, O ye elders of my church, and give ear to the voice of the living God; and attend to the words of wisdom which shall be given unto you, *according as ye have asked*" (Doctrine and Covenants 50:1; emphasis added).

A Principle, a Pattern, and Basic Imperatives

The principle of prayerful inquiry and the pattern of asking, seeking, and knocking suggest three basic imperatives for each of us as latter-day learners.

Imperative #1:
Inquiring of the Lord through asking, seeking, and knocking requires and is an expression of faith in the Savior.

True faith is focused in the Lord Jesus Christ and His attributes as the Son of God and on His mission and ministry. Such faith always leads to righteous action. The *Lectures on Faith* state that "faith [is] the first principle in revealed religion, and the foundation of all righteousness" and that it is also "the principle of action in all intelligent beings" (page 1). Action alone is not faith in the Savior, but acting in accordance with correct principles is a central component of faith. Thus, "faith without works is dead" (James 2:20).

"Faith is not only the principle of action, but of power also, in all intelligent beings, whether in heaven or on earth" (*Lectures on Faith*, 3). Thus, faith in Christ leads to righteous action, which increases our spiritual capacity and power. Understanding that faith is a principle of action and of power inspires us to exercise our moral agency in compliance with gospel truth, invites the redeeming and strengthening powers of the Savior's Atonement into our lives, enlarges the power within us whereby we are agents unto ourselves (see Doctrine and Covenants 58:28), and is essential in inviting inspiration through asking, seeking, and knocking.

Prayerful inquiry through asking, seeking, and knocking entails both holy communication and consecrated work. The blessings we seek, such as inspiration and direction from our Heavenly

Father, require some effort on our part before we can obtain them. And prayer, as a form of work, is an appointed means for obtaining the highest of all blessings (see Bible Dictionary, "Prayer," 753). We press forward and persevere in the consecrated work of prayerful inquiry after we say "amen" by acting upon the things we have expressed to Heavenly Father. We seek and knock both before and after we ask in faith.

IMPERATIVE #2:

We should be simultaneously persistent in and patient with this active process of asking, seeking, and knocking.

Note the perseverance in prayerful inquiry in the following selected scriptural examples.

"Then shall ye call upon me, and ye shall go and pray unto me, and I will hearken unto you.

"And ye shall seek me, and find me, *when ye shall search for me with all your heart*" (Jeremiah 29:12–13; emphasis added).

"And my soul hungered; and I [Enos] kneeled down before my Maker, and I cried unto him in mighty prayer and supplication for mine own soul; and *all the day long did I cry unto him;* yea, and when the night came I did still raise my voice high that it reached the heavens" (Enos 1:4; emphasis added).

"And this is not all. Do ye not suppose that I [Alma] know of these things myself? Behold, I testify unto you that I do know that these things whereof I have spoken are true. And how do ye suppose that I know of their surety?

"Behold, I say unto you they are made known unto me by the Holy Spirit of God. Behold, I have fasted and prayed *many days* that I might know these things of myself. And now I do know of myself that they are true; for the Lord God hath made them manifest unto me by his Holy Spirit; and this is the spirit of revelation which is in me" (Alma 5:45–46; emphasis added).

"Now these sons of Mosiah were with Alma at the time the angel first appeared unto him; therefore Alma did rejoice exceedingly to see his brethren; and what added more to his joy, they were still his brethren in the Lord; yea, and they had waxed strong in the knowledge of the truth; for they were men of a sound understanding and they had searched the scriptures diligently, that they might know the word of God.

"But this is not all; they had given themselves to *much* prayer, and fasting; therefore they had the spirit of prophecy, and the spirit of revelation, and when they taught, they taught with power and authority of God" (Alma 17:2–3; emphasis added).

"Yea, and when you do not cry unto the Lord, let your hearts be full, drawn out in prayer unto him *continually* for your welfare, and also for the welfare of those who are around you" (Alma 34:27; emphasis added).

"Counsel with the Lord in *all* thy doings, and he will direct thee for good; yea, when thou liest down at night lie down unto the Lord, that he may watch over you in your sleep; and when thou risest in the morning let thy heart be full of thanks unto God; and if ye do these things, ye shall be lifted up at the last day" (Alma 37:37; emphasis added).

"Behold, verily, verily, I say unto you, ye must watch and pray *always* lest ye enter into temptation; for Satan desireth to have you, that he may sift you as wheat.

"Therefore ye must *always* pray unto the Father in my name;

"And whatsoever ye shall ask the Father in my name, which is right, believing that ye shall receive, behold it shall be given unto you.

"Pray in your families unto the Father, *always* in my name, that your wives and your children may be blessed" (3 Nephi 18:18–21; emphasis added).

"And he [Jesus] commanded them that *they should not cease to pray in their hearts*" (3 Nephi 20:1; emphasis added).

"Pray *always,* that you may come off conqueror; yea, that you may conquer Satan, and that you may escape the hands of the servants of Satan that do uphold his work" (Doctrine and Covenants 10:5; emphasis added).

"Search diligently, pray *always,* and be believing, and all things shall work together for your good, if ye walk uprightly and remember the covenant wherewith ye have covenanted one with another" (Doctrine and Covenants 90:24; emphasis added).

The persistence highlighted in the preceding verses should be complemented with patience and long-suffering. The object of our prayerful inquiry should not be to present a wish list or a series of requests or demands, but to secure for ourselves and for others blessings that God is eager to bestow, according to His will and timing. Every sincere prayer is heard and answered by our Heavenly Father, but the answers we receive may not be what we expect, nor may they come to us when we want or in the way we anticipate. We must learn to "wait upon the Lord."

"The Lord is good unto them that *wait for him,* to the soul that seeketh him.

"It is good that a man should both hope and *quietly wait* for the salvation of the Lord" (Lamentations 3:25–26; emphasis added).

"*Wait on the Lord:* be of good courage, and he shall strengthen thine heart: *wait,* I say, *on the Lord*" (Psalm 27:14; emphasis added).

"*I waited patiently for the Lord;* and he inclined unto me, and heard my cry" (Psalm 40:1; emphasis added).

"But *they that wait upon the Lord* shall renew their strength; they shall mount up with wings as eagles; they shall run, and not be weary; and they shall walk, and not faint" (Isaiah 40:31; emphasis added).

"And thou shalt know that I *am* the Lord: for they shall not be ashamed that *wait for me*" (Isaiah 49:23; emphasis added).

"Therefore I will look unto the Lord; *I will wait for the God of my salvation:* my God will hear me" (Micah 7:7; emphasis added).

"Verily I say unto you my friends, fear not, let your hearts be comforted; yea, rejoice evermore, and in everything give thanks;

"*Waiting patiently on the Lord,* for your prayers have entered into the ears of the Lord of Sabaoth, and are recorded with this seal and testament—the Lord hath sworn and decreed that they shall be granted" (Doctrine and Covenants 98:1–2; emphasis added).

We always should remember to "dispute not because [we] see not, for [we] receive no witness until after the trial of [our] faith"

(Ether 12:6). Just as the prison holding Alma and Amulek did not tumble to the earth "until after their faith," and just as Ammon and his missionary brethren did not witness mighty miracles in their ministries "until after their faith" (see Ether 12:12–15), so many prayerful inquiries will not be answered "until after their faith" and will be accomplished "according to their faith in their prayers" (Doctrine and Covenants 10:47).

IMPERATIVE #3:
Discerning and accepting the will of God in our lives are fundamental elements of prayerful inquiry through asking, seeking, and knocking.

Simply saying the words "Thy will be done" is not enough. Each of us needs God's help in surrendering our will to Him.

"Prayer is the act by which the will of the Father and the will of the child are brought into correspondence with each other" (Bible Dictionary, "Prayer," 752–53). Humble, earnest, and persistent prayer enables us to recognize and align ourselves with the will of our Heavenly Father. And in this the Savior provided the perfect example as he prayed in the Garden of Gethsemane:

"Saying, Father, if thou be willing, remove this cup from me: nevertheless not my will, but thine, be done. . . .

"And being in an agony he prayed more earnestly" (Luke 22:42, 44).

Submitting our will to God's will is a theme often emphasized in the scriptures.

"*Submit* yourselves therefore to God" (James 4:7; emphasis added).

"For the natural man is an enemy to God, and has been from

the fall of Adam, and will be, forever and ever, unless he yields to the enticings of the Holy Spirit, and putteth off the natural man and becometh a saint through the atonement of Christ the Lord, and becometh as a child, submissive, meek, humble, patient, full of love, *willing to submit* to all things which the Lord seeth fit to inflict upon him, even as a child doth *submit* to his father" (Mosiah 3:19; emphasis added).

"And now it came to pass that the burdens which were laid upon Alma and his brethren were made light; yea, the Lord did strengthen them that they could bear up their burdens with ease, and they did *submit* cheerfully and with patience to all the will of the Lord" (Mosiah 24:15; emphasis added).

"And now I would that ye should be humble, and be *submissive* and gentle; easy to be entreated; full of patience and long-suffering; being temperate in all things; being diligent in keeping the commandments of God at all times; asking for whatsoever things ye stand in need, both spiritual and temporal; always returning thanks unto God for whatsoever things ye do receive" (Alma 7:23; emphasis added).

"But that ye would humble yourselves before the Lord, and call on his holy name, and watch and pray continually, that ye may not be tempted above that which ye can bear, and thus be led by the Holy Spirit, becoming humble, meek, *submissive,* patient, full of love and all long-suffering" (Alma 13:28; emphasis added).

"Nevertheless they did fast and pray oft, and did wax stronger and stronger in their humility, and firmer and firmer in the faith of Christ, unto the filling their souls with joy and consolation, yea, even to the purifying and the sanctification of their hearts, which sanctification cometh because of their *yielding* their hearts unto God" (Helaman 3:35; emphasis added).

The quintessential example of the submissiveness you and I should strive to attain in our characters is found in the relationship between Jesus and His Father.

"Yea, even so he shall be led, crucified, and slain, the flesh becoming subject even unto death, *the will of the Son being swallowed up in the will of the Father.*

"And thus God breaketh the bands of death, having gained the victory over death; giving the Son power to make intercession for the children of men—

"Having ascended into heaven, having the bowels of mercy; being filled with compassion towards the children of men; standing betwixt them and justice; having broken the bands of death, taken upon himself their iniquity and their transgressions, having redeemed them, and satisfied the demands of justice" (Mosiah 15:7–9; emphasis added).

In a similar way, prayerful inquiry through asking, seeking, and knocking that is truly efficacious requires that our individual will can be "swallowed up" in the divine will and timing of the Father and the Son.

Summary

Each and every member of The Church of Jesus Christ of Latter-day Saints has a personal responsibility to learn and live the truths of the Savior's restored gospel. The principle of prayerful inquiry and the pattern of asking, seeking, and knocking enable us to obtain the knowledge, understanding, and intelligence that are essential to becoming living members of the Lord's living Church.

"But continue thou in the things which thou hast learned and hast been assured of, knowing of whom thou hast learned them" (2 Timothy 3:14).

"Learn of me, and listen to my words; walk in the meekness of my Spirit, and you shall have peace in me" (Doctrine and Covenants 19:23).

QUESTIONS TO CONSIDER

1. What is the role of *prayerful inquiry* in fulfilling my individual responsibility as a learner?
2. What am I learning about the relationship between the *principle* of faith in the Lord Jesus Christ and the *pattern* of asking, seeking, and knocking?
3. What can and should I do to increasingly surrender *my will* to *His will?*

YOUR OWN QUESTIONS TO CONSIDER

1. _____

2. _____

3. _____

The video segments related to this chapter can be found at
desbook.com/learning

RELATED READINGS
FOR CHAPTER THREE

The principle of prayerful inquiry and the pattern of asking, seeking, and knocking are vital in obtaining the knowledge, understanding, and intelligence that are necessary for us to *know* what we need to know, to *live* as we know we should live, and to *become* what the Master would have us become—even living members of the Savior's living Church.

The following readings focus upon the importance in our daily lives of faith-filled and meaningful prayer, feasting upon the words of Christ through diligent scripture study, and the spirit of revelation.

Pray Always

From *Ensign,* November 2008, 41–44

I want to discuss three principles that can help our prayers become more meaningful, and I pray for the assistance of the Holy Ghost for me and for you.

Principle #1. Prayer becomes more meaningful as we counsel with the Lord in all our doings (see Alma 37:37).

Simply stated, prayer is communication to Heavenly Father from His sons and daughters on earth. "As soon as we learn the true relationship in which we stand toward God (namely, God is our Father, and we are his children), then at once prayer becomes natural and instinctive on our part" (Bible Dictionary, "Prayer," 752). We are commanded to pray always to the Father in the name of the Son (see 3 Nephi 18:19–20). We are promised that if we pray sincerely for that which is right and good and in accordance with God's will, we can be blessed, protected, and directed (see 3 Nephi 18:20; Doctrine and Covenants 19:38).

Revelation is communication from Heavenly Father to His children on earth. As we ask in faith, we can receive revelation upon revelation and knowledge upon knowledge and come to know the mysteries and peaceable things that bring joy and eternal life (see Doctrine and Covenants 42:61). The mysteries are those matters that can only be known and understood by the power of the Holy Ghost (see Harold B. Lee, *Ye Are the Light of the World,* 211).

The revelations of the Father and the Son are conveyed through the third member of the Godhead, even the Holy Ghost. The Holy Ghost is the witness of and messenger for the Father and the Son.

The patterns used by God in creating the earth are instructive in helping us understand how to make prayer meaningful. In the third chapter of the book of Moses we learn that all things were created spiritually before they were naturally upon the earth.

"And now, behold, I say unto you, that these are the generations of the heaven and of the earth, when they were created, in the day that I, the Lord God, made the heaven and the earth,

"And every plant of the field before it was in the earth, and every herb of the field before it grew. For I, the Lord God, created all things, of which I have spoken, spiritually, before they were naturally upon the face of the earth" (Moses 3:4–5).

We learn from these verses that the spiritual creation preceded the temporal creation. In a similar way, meaningful morning prayer is an important element in the spiritual creation of each day—and precedes the temporal creation or the actual execution of the day. Just as the temporal creation was linked to and a continuation of the spiritual creation, so meaningful morning and evening prayers are linked to and are a continuation of each other.

Consider this example. There may be things in our character, in our behavior, or concerning our spiritual growth about which we need to counsel with Heavenly Father in morning prayer. After expressing appropriate thanks for blessings received, we plead for understanding, direction, and help to do the things we cannot do in our own strength alone. For example, as we pray, we might:

- Reflect on those occasions when we have spoken harshly or inappropriately to those we love the most.

- Recognize that we know better than this, but we do not always act in accordance with what we know.
- Express remorse for our weaknesses and for not putting off the natural man more earnestly.
- Determine to pattern our life after the Savior more completely.
- Plead for greater strength to do and to become better.

Such a prayer is a key part of the spiritual preparation for our day.

During the course of the day, we keep a prayer in our heart for continued assistance and guidance—even as Alma suggested: "Let all thy thoughts be directed unto the Lord" (Alma 37:36).

We notice during this particular day that there are occasions where normally we would have a tendency to speak harshly, and we do not; or we might be inclined to anger, but we are not. We discern heavenly help and strength and humbly recognize answers to our prayer. Even in that moment of recognition, we offer a silent prayer of gratitude.

At the end of our day, we kneel again and report back to our Father. We review the events of the day and express heartfelt thanks for the blessings and the help we received. We repent and, with the assistance of the Spirit of the Lord, identify ways we can do and become better tomorrow. Thus our evening prayer builds upon and is a continuation of our morning prayer. And our evening prayer also is a preparation for meaningful morning prayer.

Morning and evening prayers—and all of the prayers in between—are not unrelated, discrete events; rather, they are linked together each day and across days, weeks, months, and even years. This is in part how we fulfill the scriptural admonition to "pray always" (Luke 21:36; 3 Nephi 18:15, 18; Doctrine and Covenants

31:12). Such meaningful prayers are instrumental in obtaining the highest blessings God holds in store for His faithful children.

Prayer becomes meaningful as we remember our relationship to Deity and heed the admonition to:

"Cry unto God for *all* thy support; yea, let *all* thy doings be unto the Lord, and whithersoever thou goest let it be in the Lord; yea, let *all* thy thoughts be directed unto the Lord; yea, let the affections of thy heart be placed upon the Lord forever.

"Counsel with the Lord in *all* thy doings, and he will direct thee for good; yea, when thou liest down at night lie down unto the Lord, that he may watch over you in your sleep; and when thou risest in the morning let thy heart be full of thanks unto God; and if ye do these things, ye shall be lifted up at the last day" (Alma 37:36–37; emphasis added).

Principle #2. Prayer becomes more meaningful as we express heartfelt gratitude.

During our service at Brigham Young University–Idaho, Sister Bednar and I frequently hosted General Authorities in our home. Our family learned an important lesson about meaningful prayer as we knelt to pray one evening with a member of the Quorum of the Twelve Apostles.

Earlier in the day Sister Bednar and I had been informed about the unexpected death of a dear friend, and our immediate desire was to pray for the surviving spouse and children. As I invited my wife to offer the prayer, the member of the Twelve, unaware of the tragedy, graciously suggested that in the prayer Sister Bednar express only appreciation for blessings received and ask for nothing. His counsel was similar to Alma's instruction to the members of the ancient Church "to pray without ceasing, and to give thanks in all things" (Mosiah 26:39). Given the unexpected tragedy, requesting blessings for our friends initially seemed to us more urgent than expressing thanks.

Sister Bednar responded in faith to the direction she received. She thanked Heavenly Father for meaningful and memorable experiences with this dear friend. She communicated sincere gratitude for the Holy Ghost as the Comforter and for the gifts of the Spirit that enable us to face adversity and to serve others. Most importantly, she expressed appreciation for the plan of salvation, for the atoning sacrifice of Jesus Christ, for His Resurrection, and for the ordinances and covenants of the restored gospel which make it possible for families to be together forever.

Our family learned from that experience a great lesson about the power of thankfulness in meaningful prayer. Because of and through that prayer, our family was blessed with inspiration about a number of issues that were pressing upon our minds and stirring in our hearts. We learned that our gratefulness for the plan of happiness and for the Savior's mission of salvation provided needed reassurance and strengthened our confidence that all would be well with our dear friends. We also received insights concerning the things about which we should pray and appropriately ask in faith.

The most meaningful and spiritual prayers I have experienced contained many expressions of thanks and few, if any, requests. As I am blessed now to pray with apostles and prophets, I find among these modern-day leaders of the Savior's Church the same characteristic that describes Captain Moroni in the Book of Mormon: these are men whose hearts swell with thanksgiving to God for the many privileges and blessings which He bestows upon His people (see Alma 48:12). Also, they do not multiply many words, for it is given unto them what they should pray, and they are filled with desire (see 3 Nephi 19:24). The prayers of prophets are childlike in their simplicity and powerful because of their sincerity.

As we strive to make our prayers more meaningful, we should remember that "in nothing doth man offend God, or against none is his wrath kindled, save those who confess not his hand in all things, and obey not his commandments" (Doctrine and Covenants 59:21). Let me recommend that periodically you and I offer a prayer in which we only give thanks and express gratitude. Ask for nothing; simply let our souls rejoice and strive to communicate appreciation with all the energy of our hearts.

Principle #3. Prayer becomes more meaningful as we pray for others with real intent and a sincere heart.

Petitioning Heavenly Father for the blessings we desire in our personal lives is good and proper. However, praying earnestly for others, both those whom we love and those who despitefully use us, is also an important element of meaningful prayer. Just as expressing gratitude more often in our prayers enlarges the conduit for revelation, so praying for others with all of the energy of our souls increases our capacity to hear and to heed the voice of the Lord.

We learn a vital lesson from the example of Lehi in the Book of Mormon. Lehi responded in faith to prophetic instruction and warnings concerning the destruction of Jerusalem. He then prayed unto the Lord "with all his heart, *in behalf of his people*" (1 Nephi 1:5; emphasis added). In answer to this fervent prayer, Lehi was blessed with a glorious vision of God and His Son and of the impending destruction of Jerusalem (see 1 Nephi 1:6–9, 13, 18). Consequently, Lehi rejoiced, and his whole heart was filled because of the things which the Lord had shown him (see 1 Nephi 1:15). Please note that the vision came in response to a prayer for others and not as a result of a request for personal edification or guidance.

The Savior is the perfect example of praying for others with real intent. In His great Intercessory Prayer uttered on the night before His Crucifixion, Jesus prayed for His Apostles and all of the Saints.

"I pray for them: I pray not for the world, but for them which thou hast given me; for they are thine. . . .

"Neither pray I for these alone, but for them also which shall believe on me through their word; . . .

" . . . that the love wherewith thou hast loved me may be in them, and I in them" (John 17:9, 20, 26).

During the Savior's ministry on the American continent, He directed the people to ponder His teachings and to pray for understanding. He healed the sick, and He prayed for the people using language that could not be written (see 3 Nephi 17:1–16). The impact of His prayer was profound: "No one can conceive of the joy which filled our souls at the time we heard him pray for us unto the Father" (3 Nephi 17:17). Imagine what it might have been like to hear the Savior of the world praying for us.

Do our spouses, children, and other family members likewise feel the power of our prayers offered unto the Father for their specific needs and desires? Do those we serve hear us pray for them with faith and sincerity? If those we love and serve have not heard and felt the influence of our earnest prayers in their behalf, then the time to repent is now. As we emulate the example of the Savior, our prayers truly will become more meaningful.

We are commanded to "pray always" (2 Nephi 32:9; Doctrine and Covenants 10:5; 90:24)—"vocally as well as in [our] heart[s]; . . . before the world as well as in secret, in public as well as in private" (Doctrine and Covenants 19:28). I testify that prayer becomes more meaningful as we counsel with the Lord in all of our doings, as we express heartfelt gratitude, and as we pray for others with real intent and a sincere heart.

A Reservoir of Living Water

From Church Educational System Fireside, February 4, 2007

What is the most valuable substance or commodity in the world? We might initially think that gold, oil, or diamonds have the greatest worth. But of all the minerals, metals, gems, and solvents found on and in the earth, the most valuable is water.

Life springs from water. Life is sustained by water. Water is the medium required to perform the various functions associated with all known forms of life. Our physical bodies are approximately two-thirds water. Whereas a person can survive for many days or even weeks without food, an individual will usually die in only three or four days without water. Most of the world's great centers of population are situated near sources of fresh water. Simply stated, life could not exist without the availability of and access to adequate supplies of clean water.

Living Water

Given the vital role of water in sustaining all forms of life, the Savior's use of the term "living water" is supernally significant. As described in the fourth chapter of John, Jesus and His disciples passed through Samaria as they were traveling from Judea to Galilee. In the city of Sychar they stopped at Jacob's well.

"There cometh a woman of Samaria to draw water: Jesus saith unto her, Give me to drink.

"(For his disciples were gone away unto the city to buy meat.)

"Then saith the woman of Samaria unto him, How is it that thou, being a Jew, askest drink of me, which am a woman of Samaria? for the Jews have no dealings with the Samaritans.

"Jesus answered and said unto her, If thou knewest the gift of God, and who it is that saith to thee, Give me to drink; thou wouldest have asked of him, and he would have given thee living water.

"The woman saith unto him, Sir, thou hast nothing to draw with, and the well is deep: from whence then hast thou that living water? . . .

"Jesus answered and said unto her, Whosoever drinketh of this water shall thirst again:

"But whosoever drinketh of the water that I shall give him shall never thirst; but the water that I shall give him shall be in him a well of water springing up into everlasting life" (John 4:7–11, 13–14).

The living water referred to in this episode is a representation of the Lord Jesus Christ and His gospel. And as water is necessary to sustain physical life, so the Savior and His doctrines, principles, and ordinances are essential for eternal life. You and I need His living water daily and in ample supply to sustain our ongoing spiritual growth and development.

The Scriptures Are a Reservoir of Living Water

The scriptures contain the words of Christ and are a reservoir of living water to which we have ready access and from which we can drink deeply and long. You and I must look to and come unto Christ, who is "the fountain of living waters" (1 Nephi 11:25; compare Ether 8:26; 12:28), by reading (see Mosiah 1:5), studying (see Doctrine and Covenants 26:1), searching (see John 5:39; Alma 17:2), and feasting (see 2 Nephi 32:3) upon the words of Christ as contained in the holy scriptures. By so doing, we can receive both spiritual direction and protection during our mortal journey.

The Church of Jesus Christ of Latter-day Saints has a sacred stewardship to preserve the written revelations in purity and in safety (see Doctrine and Covenants 42:56)—this precious reservoir of living water. A monumental work was accomplished by the Church in the 1970s and 1980s and resulted in the edition of the scriptures we enjoy today with extensive footnotes, cross-references, and additional study aids, maps, and information.

As the updated scriptures were first introduced to the members of the Church in the early 1980s, Elder Boyd K. Packer prophesied:

"With the passing of years, these scriptures will produce successive generations of faithful Christians who know the Lord Jesus Christ and are disposed to obey His will.

"The older generation has been raised without them, but there is another generation growing up" ("Scriptures," 53).

More than two decades have passed since Elder Packer spoke those words. Many Church members have only known the scriptures as we have them today. Please keep that fact in mind as I continue to quote Elder Packer:

"The revelations will be opened to them as to no other in the history of the world. Into their hands now are placed the sticks of Joseph and of Judah. They will develop a gospel scholarship beyond that which their forebears could achieve. They will have the testimony that Jesus is the Christ and be competent to proclaim Him and to defend Him" ("Scriptures," 53).

Not only are we blessed to have these scriptures so readily available to us today, but we also have the responsibility to use them consistently and effectively and to drink deeply from the reservoir of living water. I believe this generation of youth is more immersed in the scriptures, more deeply acquainted with the words of the prophets, and more prone to turn to the revelations for answers than any previous generation. But we still have a great distance to travel along the strait and narrow path—more to learn, more to apply, and more to experience.

Obtaining Living Water from the Scriptural Reservoir

I now want to review with you three basic ways or methods of obtaining living water from the scriptural reservoir: (1) *reading* the scriptures from beginning to end, (2) *studying* the scriptures by topic, and (3) *searching* the scriptures for connections, patterns, and themes. Each of these approaches can help satisfy our spiritual thirst if we invite the companionship and assistance of the Holy Ghost as we read, study, and search.

Reading a book of scripture from beginning to end initiates the flow of living water into our lives by introducing us to important stories, gospel doctrines, and timeless principles. This approach also enables us to learn about major characters in the scriptures and the sequence, timing, and context of events and teachings. Reading the written word in this way exposes us to the breadth of a volume of scripture. This is the first and most fundamental way of obtaining living water.

Studying by topic typically follows, grows out of, and builds upon our reading of the scriptures from beginning to end. For example, as we read the Book of Mormon we may identify and seek to find answers to important doctrinal and practical questions such as these:

- What is faith in the Savior?
- Why is faith in Jesus Christ the first principle of the gospel?
- Why and how does faith in the Redeemer lead to repentance?

- How does the Atonement strengthen me to do things in my daily life that I could never do with my own limited capacity and in my own strength?

Focusing upon such questions and studying by topic, using the Topical Guide and index to the triple combination, allow us to dig into and explore the depth of the scriptures and obtain a much richer spiritual knowledge. This approach increases the rate at which living water flows into our lives.

Both reading from beginning to end and studying by topic are prerequisites to the third basic method of obtaining living water from the scriptural reservoir. Whereas reading a book of scripture from beginning to end provides a basic breadth of knowledge, studying by topic increases the depth of our knowledge. *Searching* in the revelations for connections, patterns, and themes builds upon and adds to our spiritual knowledge by bringing together and expanding these first two methods; it broadens our perspective and understanding of the plan of salvation.

In my judgment, diligently searching to discover connections, patterns, and themes is in part what it means to "feast" upon the words of Christ. This approach can open the floodgates of the spiritual reservoir, enlighten our understanding through His Spirit, and produce a depth of gratitude for the holy scriptures and a degree of spiritual commitment that can be received in no other way. Such searching enables us to build upon the rock of our Redeemer and to withstand the winds of wickedness in these latter days.

I want to emphasize an essential point. You might initially assume that a person must have extensive formal education to use the methods I am describing. This assumption simply is not correct. Any honest seeker of truth, regardless of educational background, can successfully employ these simple approaches. You and I do not need sophisticated study aids and should not rely extensively upon the spiritual knowledge of others. We simply need to have a sincere desire to learn, the companionship of the Holy Ghost, the holy scriptures, and an active and inquiring mind.

The Prophet Joseph Smith taught that we should "search the Scriptures—search the revelations which we publish, and ask your Heavenly Father, in the name of His Son Jesus Christ, to manifest the truth unto you, and if you do it with an eye single to His glory, nothing doubting, He will answer you by the power of His Holy Spirit. You will then know for yourselves and not for another. You will not then be dependent on man for the knowledge of God" (in *History of the Church,* 1:282).

If you and I will ask, seek, and knock (see Matthew 7:7), always keeping ourselves worthy to learn from the Spirit, then the gates of the spiritual reservoir will open to us and the living water will flow. I witness, I testify, and I promise that this is true.

Let me briefly explain and provide examples of what I mean by connections, patterns, and themes.

Connections

A connection is a relationship or link between ideas, people, things, or events, and the scriptures are full of connections. Consider the relationship between the Eternal Father and His Son, Jesus Christ (see Mosiah 15:1–9); between mercy and grace (see 2 Nephi 9:8); between clean hands and a pure heart (see Psalm 24:4); between a broken heart and a contrite spirit (see 3 Nephi 9:20); between the wheat and the tares (see Doctrine and Covenants 101:65); between knowledge and intelligence (see Doctrine and Covenants 130:18–19); between justification and sanctification (see Doctrine and Covenants 20:30–31); between sheep and goats (see Matthew 25:32–33); between immortality and eternal life (see Moses 1:39); and countless others. Prayerfully identifying, learning about, and pondering such connections—the similarities and differences, for example—is a primary source of living water and yields inspired insights and treasures of hidden knowledge.

As I have read each of the standard works from beginning to end and studied different topics, I noticed that the word *understanding* was commonly described in relation to the heart. Two verses in the Book of Mormon illustrate this connection:

"Ye have not applied your *hearts* to *understanding;* therefore, ye have not been wise" (Mosiah 12:27; emphasis added).

"And the multitude did hear and do bear record; and their hearts were open and they did *understand* in their *hearts* the words which he prayed" (3 Nephi 19:33; emphasis added).

I find it most interesting in these and many other verses that understanding is linked primarily to the heart. Note that we are not explicitly counseled to apply our minds to understanding. Obviously, we must use our minds and our rational capacity to obtain and evaluate information and to reach appropriate conclusions and judgments. But perhaps the scriptures are suggesting to us that reason and "the arm of the flesh" (Doctrine and Covenants 1:19) are not sufficient to produce true understanding. Thus, understanding, as the word is used in the scriptures, does not refer solely or even primarily to intellectual or cognitive comprehension. Rather, understanding occurs when what we know in our minds is confirmed as true in our hearts by the witness of the Holy Ghost.

The spiritual gift of revelation most typically operates as thoughts and feelings put into our minds and hearts by the Holy Ghost (see Doctrine and Covenants 8:2–3; 100:5–8). And as testimony and conviction move from our heads to our hearts, we no longer just have information or knowledge—but we begin to understand and seek after the mighty change of heart. Understanding, then, is the result of revelation; it is a spiritual gift, it is a prerequisite to conversion, and it entices us to more consistently live in accordance with the principles we are learning.

This revealed insight about the relationship between the heart and understanding has greatly influenced my approach to gospel learning and study, has affected positively the way Sister Bednar and I teach our children and grandchildren, and has impacted my priesthood service.

Patterns

A pattern is a plan, model, or standard that can be used as a guide for repetitively doing or making something. And the scriptures are full of spiritual patterns. Typically, a scriptural pattern is broader and more comprehensive than a connection. In the Doctrine and Covenants we find patterns for preaching the gospel (see Doctrine and Covenants 50:13–29), for avoiding deception (see Doctrine and Covenants 52:14, 18–19), for constructing temples (see Doctrine and Covenants 115:14–16), for establishing cities (see Doctrine and Covenants 94), for organizing priesthood quorums (see Doctrine and Covenants 107:85–100) and high councils (see Doctrine and Covenants 102:12), and for a variety of other purposes. Identifying and studying scriptural patterns is another important source of living water and helps us become acquainted and more familiar with the wisdom and the mind of the Lord (see Doctrine and Covenants 95:13).

As I have both read from beginning to end and studied topics in the Doctrine and Covenants, I have been impressed with a pattern that is evident in many of the Lord's responses to the questions of missionaries. On a number of occasions in 1831, various groups of elders who had been called to preach the gospel desired to know how they should proceed and by what route and manner they should travel. In revelations given through the Prophet Joseph Smith, the Lord respectively counseled these brethren that they could travel on water or by land (see Doctrine and Covenants 61:22), that they could make or purchase the needed vehicles (see Doctrine and Covenants 60:5), that they could travel all together or go two by two (see Doctrine and Covenants 62:5), and that they could appropriately travel in a number of different directions (see Doctrine and Covenants 80:3). The revelations specifically instructed the brethren to make these decisions "as seemeth you good" (Doctrine and Covenants 60:5; 62:5) or "as it is made known unto them according to their judgments" (Doctrine and Covenants 61:22). And in each of these instances the Savior declared, "It mattereth not unto me" (Doctrine and Covenants 60:5; 61:22; 62:5; 63:40; see also 80:3).

The Lord's statement that such things "mattereth not unto me" initially may seem surprising. Clearly, the Savior was not saying to these missionaries that He did not care about what they were doing. Rather, He was emphasizing the importance of putting first things first and focusing upon the right things—which, in these instances, were getting to the assigned field of labor and initiating the work. They were to exercise faith, use good judgment, act in accordance with the direction of the Spirit, and determine the best way to travel to their assignments. The essential thing was the work they had been called to perform; how they got there was important but was not essential.

What a remarkable pattern for you and for me to apply in our lives. Jesus Christ knows and loves us individually. He is concerned about our spiritual development and progress, and He encourages us to grow through the exercise of inspired, righteous, and wise judgment. The Redeemer will never leave us alone. We should always pray for guidance and direction. We should always seek for the constant companionship of the Holy Ghost. But we should not be dismayed or discouraged if answers to our petitions for direction or help do not necessarily come quickly. Such answers rarely come all at once. Our progress would be hindered and our judgment would be weak if every answer was given to us immediately and without requiring the price of faith, work, study, and persistence.

The pattern I am describing is illustrated succinctly in the following instruction to those early missionaries:

"I, the Lord, am willing, if any among you desire, to ride upon horses, or upon mules, or in chariots, he shall receive this blessing, if he receive it from the hand of the Lord, with *a thankful heart in all things.*

"These things remain with you to do *according to judgment and the directions of the Spirit.*

"Behold, the kingdom is yours. And behold, and lo, *I am with the faithful always.* Even so. Amen" (Doctrine and Covenants 62:7–9; emphasis added).

The principal issues in this episode are not horses, mules, or chariots; rather, they are gratitude, judgment, and faithfulness. Please note the basic elements in this pattern: (1) a thankful heart in all things; (2) act according to judgment and the directions of the Spirit; and (3) the Savior is with the faithful always. Can we begin to sense the direction and assurance, the renewal and strength that can come from following this simple pattern for inspired and righteous judgment? Truly, scriptural patterns are a precious source of living water.

The most demanding judgments we ever make are seldom between good or bad or between attractive and unattractive alternatives. Usually, our toughest choices are between good and good. In this scriptural episode, horses, mules, and chariots may have been equally effective options for missionary travel. In a similar way, you and I also might identify at various times in our lives more than one acceptable opportunity or option that we could choose to pursue. We should remember this pattern from the scriptures as we approach such important decisions. If we put essential things first in our lives—things such as dedicated discipleship, honoring covenants, and keeping the commandments—then we will be blessed with inspiration and strong judgment as we pursue the path that leads us back to our heavenly home. If we put essential things first, we "cannot go amiss" (Doctrine and Covenants 80:3).

Themes

Themes are overarching, recurring, and unifying qualities or ideas, like essential threads woven throughout a text. Generally, scriptural themes are broader and more comprehensive than patterns or connections. In fact, themes provide the background and context for understanding connections and patterns. The process of searching for and identifying scriptural themes leads us to the fundamental doctrines and principles of salvation—to the eternal truths that invite the confirming witness of the Holy Ghost (see 1 John 5:6). This approach to obtaining living water from the scriptural reservoir is the most demanding and rigorous; it also yields the greatest edification and spiritual refreshment. And the scriptures are replete with powerful themes.

For example, the Book of Mormon came forth in this dispensation to "the convincing of the Jew and Gentile that Jesus is the Christ, the Eternal God, manifesting himself unto all nations" (Book of Mormon title page). The central and recurring theme of the Book of Mormon is the invitation for all to "come unto Christ, and be perfected in him" (Moroni 10:32). The teachings, warnings, admonitions, and episodes in this remarkable book of scripture all focus upon and testify of Jesus the Christ as the Redeemer and our Savior.

Let me provide a few additional examples of important themes using scriptures from the Book of Mormon:

"If . . . the children of men keep the commandments of God he doth nourish them, and strengthen them, and provide means whereby they can accomplish the thing which he has commanded them" (1 Nephi 17:3).

"Press forward with a steadfastness in Christ" (2 Nephi 31:20).

"Men are, that they might have joy" (2 Nephi 2:25).

"In the strength of the Lord thou canst do all things" (Alma 20:4).

"Wickedness never was happiness" (Alma 41:10).

If you promise not to laugh, I will tell you about one of the simple ways I search for scriptural themes. I do not advocate or recommend that you use the same approach; different people use different methods with equal effectiveness. I am simply describing a process that works well for me.

In preparation for a speaking assignment, I was impressed to talk about the spirit and purposes of gathering. I had been studying and pondering Elder Russell M. Nelson's recent conference message on the principle of gathering (see "The Gathering of Scattered Israel," 79–82), and the topic was perfectly suited to the nature of and setting for my assignment.

I recognized that I had much to learn from the scriptures about gathering. So I identified and made copies of every scripture in the standard works that included any form of the word *gather*. I next read each scripture, looking for connections, patterns, and themes. It is important to note that I did not start my reading with a preconceived set of things for which I was looking. I prayed for the assistance of the Holy Ghost and simply started reading.

As I reviewed the scriptures about gathering, I marked verses with similar phrases or points of emphasis, using a colored pencil. By the time I had read all of the scriptures, some of the verses were marked in red, some were marked in green, and some were marked in other colors.

Now, here comes the part that may make you laugh. I next used my scissors to cut out the scriptures I had copied and sorted them into piles by color. The process produced a large pile of scriptures marked with red, a large pile of scriptures marked with green, and so forth. I then sorted the scriptures within each large pile into smaller piles. As a first grader I must have really liked cutting with scissors and putting things into piles!

The results of this process taught me a great deal about the principle of gathering. For example, I learned from examining my large piles that the scriptures describe at least three key aspects of gathering: the *purposes* of gathering, the *types and places* of gathering, and the *blessings* of gathering.

I noted that some of the primary *purposes* of gathering are to worship (see Mosiah 18:25), to receive counsel and instruction (see Mosiah 18:7), to build up the Church (see Doctrine and Covenants 101:63–64), and to provide defense and protection (see Doctrine and Covenants 115:6). In studying about the *types and places* of gathering, I discovered that we are gathered into eternal families (see Mosiah 2:5), into the restored Church (see Doctrine and Covenants 101:64–65), into stakes of Zion (see Doctrine and Covenants 109:59), into holy temples (see Alma 26:5–6), and into two great centers: old Jerusalem (see Ether 13:11) and the city of Zion or New Jerusalem (see Doctrine and Covenants 42:9; Articles of Faith 1:10). I was grateful to learn that edification (see Ephesians 4:12–13), preservation (see Moses 7:61), and strength (see Doctrine and Covenants 82:14) are some of the *blessings* of gathering.

Through this process I gained an even deeper appreciation for the spirit of gathering as an integral part of the restoration of all things in the dispensation of the fulness of times.

The Blessings We Can Receive

The blessings of knowledge, understanding, revelation, and spiritual exhilaration that we can receive as we read, study, and search the scriptures are marvelous. "Feasting upon the word of Christ" (2 Nephi 31:20) is edifying, exciting, and enjoyable. The word is good, "for it beginneth to enlarge my soul; yea, it beginneth to enlighten my understanding, yea, it beginneth to be delicious to me" (Alma 32:28). "Behold they are written, ye have them before you, therefore search them" (3 Nephi 20:11), and they "shall be in [you] a well of water springing up into everlasting life" (John 4:14).

In my personal reading, studying, and searching over a period of years, I have focused many times upon the doctrine of the Atonement of Jesus Christ. No event, knowledge, or influence has had a greater impact upon me than repeatedly reading about, studying in depth, and searching for connections, patterns, and themes related to the doctrine of the Atonement. This central, saving doctrine, over time, gradually has distilled upon my soul as the dews from heaven; has influenced my thoughts, words, and deeds (see Mosiah 4:30); and literally has become for me a well of living water.

Lehi's Vision

The importance of reading, studying, and searching the scriptures is highlighted in several elements of Lehi's vision of the tree of life.

Father Lehi saw several groups of people pressing forward along the strait and narrow path, seeking to obtain the tree and its fruit.

The members of each group had entered onto the path through the gate of repentance and baptism by water and had received the gift of the Holy Ghost (see 2 Nephi 31:17–20). The tree of life is the central feature in the dream and is identified in 1 Nephi 11 as a representation of Jesus Christ. The fruit on the tree is a symbol for the blessings of the Savior's Atonement. Interestingly, the major theme of the Book of Mormon, inviting all to come unto Christ, is central in Lehi's vision. Of particular interest is the rod of iron that led to the tree (see 1 Nephi 8:19). The rod of iron is the word of God.

In 1 Nephi 8, verses 21 through 23, we learn about a group of people who pressed forward and commenced in the path that led to the tree of life. However, as the people encountered the mist of darkness, which represents the temptations of the devil (see 1 Nephi 12:17), they lost their way, they wandered off, and they were lost.

It is important to note that no mention is made about the rod of iron in these verses. Those who ignore or treat lightly the word of God do not have access to that divine compass which points the way to the Savior. Consider that this group obtained the path and pressed forward, exhibiting a measure of faith in Christ and spiritual conviction, but they were diverted by the temptations of the devil and were lost.

In verses 24 through 28 of chapter 8 we read about a second group of people who obtained the strait and narrow path that led to the tree of life. This group pressed forward through the mist of darkness, clinging to the rod of iron even until they did come forth and partake of the fruit of the tree. However, as this second group of people was mocked by the occupants of the great and spacious building, they were ashamed and fell away into forbidden paths and were lost. Please notice that this group is described as *clinging* to the rod of iron.

It is significant that the second group pressed forward with faith and commitment. They also had the added blessing of the rod of iron, *and they were clinging to it!* However, as they were confronted with persecution and adversity, they fell away into forbidden paths and were lost. Even with faith, commitment, and the word of God, this group was lost—perhaps because they only *periodically* read *or* studied *or* searched the scriptures. Clinging to the rod of iron suggests to me only occasional "bursts" of study or irregular dipping rather than consistent, ongoing immersion in the word of God.

In verse 30 we read about a third group of people who pressed forward continually holding fast to the rod of iron until they came forth and fell down and partook of the fruit of the tree. The key phrase in this verse is "continually holding fast" to the rod of iron.

The third group also pressed forward with faith and conviction; however, there is no indication that they wandered off, fell into forbidden paths, or were lost. Perhaps this third group of people *consistently* read *and* studied *and* searched the words of Christ. Perhaps it was the constant flow of living water that saved the third group from perishing. This is the group you and I should strive to join.

"What meaneth the rod of iron which our father saw, that led to the tree?

"And I said unto them that it was the word of God; and whoso would hearken unto the word of God, and would *hold fast unto it,* they would never perish; neither could the temptations and the fiery darts of the adversary overpower them unto blindness, to lead them away to destruction" (1 Nephi 15:23–24; emphasis added).

What, then, is the difference between clinging and holding fast to the rod of iron? Let me suggest that holding fast to the iron rod entails the prayerful and consistent use of all three of the ways of obtaining living water that we have discussed.

"And it came to pass that I beheld that the rod of iron, which my father had seen, was the word of God, which led to the fountain of living waters, or to the tree of life" (1 Nephi 11:25).

Each of these approaches—reading from beginning to end, studying by topic, and searching for connections, patterns, and themes—is edifying, is instructive, and provides an intermittent portion of the Savior's living water. I believe, however, that the regular use of all three methods produces a more constant flow of living water and is in large measure what it means to hold fast to the rod of iron.

Through normal activity each day, you and I lose a substantial amount of the water that constitutes so much of our physical bodies. Thirst is a demand by the cells of the body for water, and the water in our bodies must be replenished daily. It frankly does not make sense to occasionally "fill up" with water, with long periods of dehydration in between. The same thing is true spiritually. Spiritual thirst is a need for living water. A constant flow of living water is far superior to sporadic sipping.

Are you and I daily reading, studying, and searching the scriptures in a way that enables us to hold fast to the rod of iron—or are you and I merely clinging? Are you and I pressing forward toward the fountain of living waters—relying upon the word of God? These are important questions for each of us to ponder prayerfully.

I witness of Jesus Christ and of the power of His word and of Him as the Word. He is the Son of the Eternal Father, and I know that He lives. I testify that holding fast to the rod of iron will lead to His living water. May we ever remember that

When temptation's power is nigh,
Our pathway clouded o'er,
Upon the rod we can rely,
And heaven's aid implore.
(Hymns, no. 274)

The Spirit of Revelation

From *Ensign,* May 2011, 87–90

I invite you to consider two experiences most of us have had with light.

The first experience occurred as we entered a dark room and turned on a light switch. Remember how in an instant a bright flood of illumination filled the room and caused the darkness to disappear. What previously had been unseen and uncertain became clear and recognizable. This experience was characterized by immediate and intense recognition of light.

The second experience took place as we watched night turn into morning. Do you recall the slow and almost imperceptible increase in light on the horizon? In contrast to turning on a light in a dark room, the light from the rising sun did not immediately burst forth. Rather, gradually and steadily the intensity of the light increased, and the darkness of night was replaced by the radiance of morning. Eventually, the sun did dawn over the skyline. But the visual evidence of the sun's impending arrival was apparent hours before the sun actually appeared over the horizon. This experience was characterized by subtle and gradual discernment of light.

From these two ordinary experiences with light, we can learn much about the spirit of revelation. I pray the Holy Ghost will inspire and instruct us as we now focus upon the spirit of revelation and basic patterns whereby revelation is received.

The Spirit of Revelation

Revelation is communication from God to His children on the earth and one of the great blessings associated with the gift and constant companionship of the Holy Ghost. The Prophet Joseph Smith taught, "The Holy Ghost is a revelator," and "no man can receive the Holy Ghost without receiving revelations" (*Teachings: Joseph Smith,* 132).

The spirit of revelation is available to every person who receives by proper priesthood authority the saving ordinances of baptism by immersion for the remission of sins and the laying on of hands for the gift of the Holy Ghost—and who is acting in faith to fulfill the priesthood injunction to "receive the Holy Ghost." This blessing is not restricted to the presiding authorities of the Church; rather, it belongs to and should be operative in the life of every man, woman, and child who reaches the age of accountability and enters into sacred covenants. Sincere desire and worthiness invite the spirit of revelation into our lives.

Joseph Smith and Oliver Cowdery gained valuable experience with the spirit of revelation as they translated the Book of Mormon. These brethren learned they could receive whatever knowledge was necessary to complete their work if they asked in faith, with an honest heart, believing they would receive. And over time they increasingly understood the spirit of revelation typically functions as thoughts and feelings that come into our minds and hearts by the power of the Holy Ghost (see Doctrine and Covenants 8:1–2; 100:5–8). As the Lord instructed them: "Now, behold, this is the spirit of revelation; behold, this is the spirit by which Moses brought the children of Israel through the Red Sea on dry ground. Therefore this is thy gift; apply unto it" (Doctrine and Covenants 8:3–4).

I emphasize the phrase "apply unto it" in relation to the spirit of revelation. In the scriptures, the influence of the Holy Ghost frequently is described as "a still small voice" (1 Kings 19:12; 1 Nephi 17:45; see also 3 Nephi 11:3) and a "voice of perfect mildness" (Helaman 5:30). Because the Spirit whispers to us gently and delicately, it is easy to understand why we should shun inappropriate media, pornography, and harmful, addictive substances and behaviors. These tools of the adversary can impair and eventually destroy our capacity to recognize and respond to the subtle messages from God delivered by the power of His Spirit. Each of us should consider seriously and ponder prayerfully how we can reject the devil's enticements and righteously "apply unto it," even the spirit of revelation, in our personal lives and families.

Patterns of Revelation

Revelations are conveyed in a variety of ways, including, for example, dreams, visions, conversations with heavenly messengers, and inspiration. Some revelations are received immediately and intensely; some are recognized gradually and subtly. The two experiences with light I described help us to better understand these two basic patterns of revelation.

A light turned on in a dark room is like receiving a message from God quickly, completely, and all at once. Many of us have experienced this pattern of revelation as we have been given answers to sincere prayers or been provided with needed direction or protection, according to God's will and timing. Descriptions of such immediate and intense manifestations are found in the scriptures, recounted in Church history, and evidenced in our own lives. Indeed, these mighty miracles do occur. However, this pattern of revelation tends to be more rare than common.

The gradual increase of light radiating from the rising sun is like receiving a message from God "line upon line, precept upon precept" (2 Nephi 28:30). Most frequently, revelation comes in small increments over time and is granted according to our desire, worthiness, and preparation. Such communications from Heavenly Father gradually and gently "distil upon [our souls] as the dews from heaven" (Doctrine and Covenants 121:45). This pattern of revelation tends to be more common than rare and is evident in the experiences of Nephi as he tried several different approaches before successfully obtaining the plates of brass from Laban (see 1 Nephi 3–4). Ultimately, he was led by the Spirit to Jerusalem, "not knowing beforehand the things which [he] should do" (1 Nephi 4:6). And he did not learn how to build a ship of curious workmanship all at one time; rather, Nephi was shown by the Lord "from time to time after what manner [he] should work the timbers of the ship" (1 Nephi 18:1).

Both the history of the Church and our personal lives are replete with examples of the Lord's pattern for receiving revelation "line upon line, precept upon precept." For example, the fundamental truths of the restored gospel were not delivered to the Prophet Joseph Smith all at once in the Sacred Grove. These priceless treasures were revealed as circumstances warranted and as the timing was right.

President Joseph F. Smith explained how this pattern of revelation occurred in his life: "As a boy . . . I would frequently . . . ask the Lord to show me some marvelous thing, in order that I might receive a testimony. But the Lord withheld marvels from me, and showed me the truth, line upon line . . . , until He made me to know the truth from the crown of my head to the soles of my feet, and until doubt and fear had been absolutely purged from me. He did not have to send an angel from the heavens to do this, nor did

He have to speak with the trump of an archangel. By the whisperings of the still small voice of the spirit of the living God, He gave to me the testimony I possess. And by this principle and power He will give to all the children of men a knowledge of the truth that will stay with them, and it will make them to know the truth, as God knows it, and to do the will of the Father as Christ does it. And no amount of marvelous manifestations will ever accomplish this" (in Conference Report, April 1900, 40–41).

We as members of the Church tend to emphasize marvelous and dramatic spiritual manifestations so much that we may fail to appreciate and may even overlook the customary pattern by which the Holy Ghost accomplishes His work. The very "simpleness of the way" (1 Nephi 17:41) of receiving small and incremental spiritual impressions that over time and in totality constitute a desired answer or the direction we need may cause us to look "beyond the mark" (Jacob 4:14).

I have talked with many individuals who question the strength of their personal testimony and underestimate their spiritual capacity because they do not receive frequent, miraculous, or strong impressions. Perhaps as we consider the experiences of Joseph in the Sacred Grove, of Saul on the road to Damascus, and of Alma the Younger, we come to believe something is wrong with or lacking in us if we fall short in our lives of these well-known and spiritually striking examples. If you have had similar thoughts or doubts, please know that you are quite normal. Just keep pressing forward obediently and with faith in the Savior. As you do so, you "cannot go amiss" (Doctrine and Covenants 80:3).

President Joseph F. Smith counseled: "Show me Latter-day Saints who have to feed upon miracles, signs and visions in order to keep them steadfast in the Church, and I will show you members . . . who are not in good standing before God, and who are walking in slippery paths. It is not by marvelous manifestations unto us that we shall be established in the truth, but it is by humility and faithful obedience to the commandments and laws of God" (in Conference Report, April 1900, 40).

Another common experience with light helps us learn an additional truth about the "line upon line, precept upon precept" pattern of revelation. Sometimes the sun rises on a morning that is cloudy or foggy. Because of the overcast conditions, perceiving the light is more difficult, and identifying the precise moment when the sun rises over the horizon is not possible. But on such a morning we nonetheless have sufficient light to recognize a new day and to conduct our affairs.

In a similar way, we many times receive revelation without recognizing precisely how or when we are receiving revelation. An important episode from Church history illustrates this principle.

In the spring of 1829, Oliver Cowdery was a schoolteacher in Palmyra, New York. As he learned about Joseph Smith and the work of translating the Book of Mormon, Oliver felt impressed to offer his assistance to the young prophet. Consequently, he traveled to Harmony, Pennsylvania, and became Joseph's scribe. The timing of his arrival and the help he provided were vital to the coming forth of the Book of Mormon.

The Savior subsequently revealed to Oliver that as often as he had prayed for guidance, he had received direction from the Spirit of the Lord. "If it had not been so," the Lord declared, "thou wouldst not have come to the place where thou art at this time. Behold, thou knowest that thou hast inquired of me and I did enlighten thy mind; and now I tell thee these things that thou mayest know that thou hast been enlightened by the Spirit of truth" (Doctrine and Covenants 6:14–15).

Thus, Oliver received a revelation through the Prophet Joseph

Smith informing him that he had been receiving revelation. Apparently Oliver had not recognized how and when he had been receiving direction from God and needed this instruction to increase his understanding about the spirit of revelation. In essence, Oliver had been walking in the light as the sun was rising on a cloudy morning.

In many of the uncertainties and challenges we encounter in our lives, God requires us to do our best, to act and not be acted upon (see 2 Nephi 2:26), and to trust in Him. We may not see angels, hear heavenly voices, or receive overwhelming spiritual impressions. We frequently may press forward hoping and praying—but without absolute assurance—that we are acting in accordance with God's will. But as we honor our covenants and keep the commandments, as we strive ever more consistently to do good and to become better, we can walk with the confidence that God will guide our steps. And we can speak with the assurance that God will inspire our utterances. This is in part the meaning of the scripture that declares, "Then shall thy confidence wax strong in the presence of God" (Doctrine and Covenants 121:45).

As you appropriately seek for and apply unto the spirit of revelation, I promise you will "walk in the light of the Lord" (Isaiah 2:5; 2 Nephi 12:5). Sometimes the spirit of revelation will operate immediately and intensely, other times subtly and gradually, and often so delicately you may not even consciously recognize it. But regardless of the pattern whereby this blessing is received, the light it provides will illuminate and enlarge your soul, enlighten your understanding (see Alma 5:7; 32:28), and direct and protect you and your family.

CHAPTER FOUR

Doctrines, Principles, and Applications: A Framework for Gospel Learning

Learning is central to the plan of salvation, to our happiness in mortality, and to our eternal progress. In this chapter, a basic and flexible framework for learning about gospel learning is introduced and explained. The framework includes three basic elements: doctrines, principles, and applications.

Doctrines

A gospel doctrine is a truth—a truth of salvation revealed by a loving Heavenly Father. Gospel doctrines are eternal, do not change, and pertain to the eternal progression and exaltation of Heavenly Father's sons and daughters. Doctrines such as the nature of the Godhead, the plan of happiness, and the Atonement of Jesus Christ are foundational, fundamental, and comprehensive. The core doctrines of the gospel of Jesus Christ are relatively few in number.

Gospel doctrines answer the question of "why?" For example, the doctrine of the plan of happiness answers the questions of *why* we are here upon the earth, *why* marriage between a man and a woman is ordained of God, and *why* the family is central to the Creator's plan for the eternal destiny of His children. The doctrine of the Godhead helps us to understand *why* we are to become perfect even as our Father in Heaven and His Son Jesus Christ are perfect (see Matthew 5:48; 3 Nephi 12:48). The doctrine of the Atonement explains *why* Jesus Christ is our mediator and advocate with the Father (see 1 Timothy 2:5; Doctrine and Covenants 45:3).

The doctrines of the restored gospel are found in the standard works of The Church of Jesus Christ of Latter-day Saints, in the teachings of the living prophets and apostles, and in the authorized declarations and proclamations of the First Presidency and the Quorum of the Twelve Apostles. Ultimately, however, only the President of the Church and the Quorum of the First Presidency have the authority to define the doctrines of the Church.

Each of the first three articles of faith emphasizes a fundamental doctrine of the restored gospel of Jesus Christ. Both the content and sequence of the doctrines presented in the articles of faith are instructive. For example, the first article of faith focuses upon the Godhead.

"We believe in God, the Eternal Father, and in His Son, Jesus Christ, and in the Holy Ghost" (Articles of Faith 1:1).

The second article of faith highlights the plan of salvation and the role of the Atonement in overcoming the consequences of the fall of Adam.

"We believe that men will be punished for their own sins, and not for Adam's transgression" (Articles of Faith 1:2).

And the third article of faith focuses upon the plan of salvation and the role of the Savior's Atonement in overcoming our individual sins and mortal weaknesses.

"We believe that through the Atonement of Christ, all mankind may be saved, by obedience to the laws and ordinances of the Gospel" (Articles of Faith 1:3).

Gospel doctrines are a supernal source of power and influence for good. President Boyd K. Packer has explained:

See video segment 6

"True doctrine, understood, changes attitudes and behavior. The study of the doctrines of the gospel will improve behavior quicker than a study of behavior will improve behavior. Preoccupation with unworthy behavior can lead to unworthy behavior. That is why we stress so forcefully the study of the doctrines of the gospel" ("Little Children," 17).

Two important words in President Packer's statement should be highlighted. First, *true* doctrine changes attitudes and behavior. *True* suggests doctrine that comes from God and is correct and accurate. The sources of such doctrine are the authorized teachings of the Lord's anointed servants and the scriptures. False doctrines, personal opinions and speculation, and gospel "hobbies" do not and cannot produce the same righteous effect upon our outlook and conduct.

Second, true doctrine that is *understood* changes attitudes and behavior. Interestingly, President Packer did not teach that simply knowing true doctrine changes us. Rather, doctrine must be understood. As we discussed in chapter 2, the word *understanding* in the scriptures frequently is linked to and associated with the heart and refers to a revealed result or conclusion. Thus, true doctrine confirmed in the heart as true by the witness of the Holy Ghost changes attitudes and behavior. Knowing true doctrine is necessary but is not sufficient. Understanding true doctrine both in our minds and in our hearts is essential to righteous attitudes and actions.

Basic gospel doctrines are the spiritual foundation for all that we learn, teach, and do—and a vital source of power and strength as we strive to become what the Lord would have us become. For example, the eternal importance of gender and of eternal marriage can be properly understood only within the context of our Heavenly Father's plan of happiness. Emphasizing the institution of marriage without linking it adequately to the simple and fundamental doctrine of the plan cannot provide sufficient direction, protection, and hope in a world confused about these vital issues. A knowledge and testimony of the plan of salvation lead men and women to hope and prepare for marriage in the house of the Lord, strengthen their commitment to honor the covenant of eternal marriage, and overcome fear and uncertainty that cause some to avoid or postpone marriage. As we learn from the teachings of Alma, God gave unto the children of men commandments *after* having made known unto them the plan of redemption (see Alma 12:32).

In the times in which we do now and will yet live, only the restored gospel of Jesus Christ provides the answers to the eternally important *why* questions—the questions of the soul. Answers to all of the *why* questions we might ask have not been revealed, but the answers to the most fundamental *why* questions are readily available in the doctrine of Christ.

Principles

A gospel principle is a doctrinally based guideline for the righteous exercise of moral agency. Principles are subsets or components of broader gospel truths. Principles provide direction. Correct principles always are based upon and arise from doctrines, do not change, and answer the question of "what?" Many principles can grow out of and be associated with a single doctrine, as illustrated in Figure 1.

DOCTRINES	Nature of the Godhead	Plan of Happiness	Atonement
PRINCIPLES	love unity prayer	obedience service progress and become	faith in Christ repentance endure valiantly to the end

Figure 1

A principle is not a behavior or a specific action. Rather, principles provide basic guidelines for behavior and action. For example, the fourth article of faith states,

"We believe that the first *principles* and ordinances of the Gospel are: first, Faith in the Lord Jesus Christ; second, Repentance; third, Baptism by immersion for the remission of sins; fourth, Laying on of hands for the gift of the Holy Ghost" (Articles of Faith 1:4; emphasis added).

The first three articles of faith identify fundamental doctrines of the restored gospel. The fourth article of faith, however, links principles—as guidelines of what to do—to doctrine. The first two principles that flow from the doctrine of the Atonement are faith in the Lord Jesus Christ and repentance. The Atonement explains the *why,* and the principles focus upon the *what.* Thus, the principles of faith in Christ and repentance provide the necessary guidance so the Atonement can become efficacious in our lives.

Elder Dallin H. Oaks illustrated the importance of principles in his teaching to the Aaronic Priesthood holders of the Church in a general conference priesthood meeting. He described the principle of non-distraction and indicated that a holder of the Aaronic Priesthood would never want to do anything in appearance or behavior that would distract any member of the Church from his or her worship and renewal of covenants. He also emphasized the related principles of orderliness, cleanliness, reverence, and dignity.

Interestingly, Elder Oaks did not provide for the young men a lengthy list of things "to do" and "not to do." Rather, he explained the principle with the expectation that the young men and their parents and teachers could and should use their own judgment and inspiration to follow the guideline.

"I will not suggest detailed rules, since the circumstances in various wards and branches in our worldwide Church are so different that a specific rule that seems required in one setting may be inappropriate in another. Rather, I will suggest a principle based on the doctrines. If all understand this principle and act in harmony with it, there should be little need for rules. If rules or counseling are needed in individual cases, local leaders can provide them, consistent with the doctrines and their related principles" ("The Aaronic Priesthood and the Sacrament," 39).

The Prophet Joseph Smith emphasized the guiding power of principles when he was asked how he was able to lead and govern the Latter-day Saints so effectively. He answered, "I teach them correct principles, and they govern themselves" (quoted by John Taylor, *Millennial Star,* 15 November 1851, 339).

APPLICATIONS

Applications are the actual behaviors, action steps, practices, or procedures by which gospel doctrines and principles are enacted in our lives. Whereas doctrines and principles do not change, applications appropriately can vary according to needs and circumstances. Applications answer the question of "how." Many applications can grow out of and be associated with a single principle. In Figure 2, please note the large number of behaviors and specific action steps that grow out of the principle of faith in the Lord Jesus Christ.

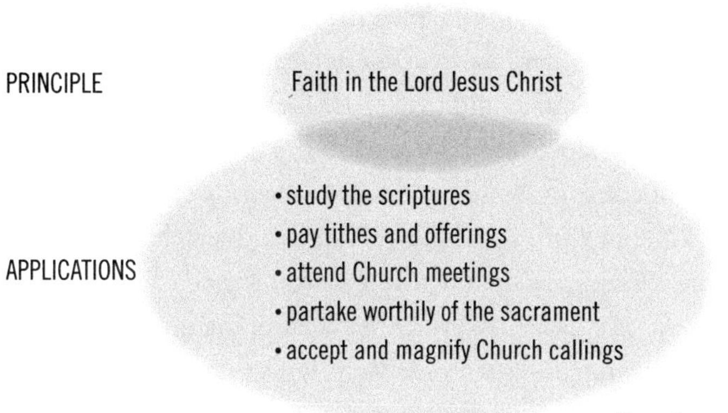

PRINCIPLE   Faith in the Lord Jesus Christ

APPLICATIONS
- study the scriptures
- pay tithes and offerings
- attend Church meetings
- partake worthily of the sacrament
- accept and magnify Church callings

Figure 2

The principle of non-distraction as taught by Elder Oaks, for example, can be applied appropriately as Aaronic Priesthood holders avoid extremes in clothing, haircuts, speech, and behavior. The potential and specific types of distractions to be avoided obviously may vary from Alabama to Africa to Argentina. Although the principle always remains the same, the applications may vary according to need and circumstances.

USING THE FRAMEWORK

The framework of doctrines, principles, and applications is a flexible tool that can be used to enhance our gospel learning and can be a useful aid as we apply the principle of prayerful inquiry and the pattern of asking, seeking, and knocking.

Please do not view and use the framework as a rigid set of definitions or as a formula that leads to "correct" answers about which applications and principles are associated with particular gospel doctrines. In fact, some readers may eagerly anticipate an appendix at the end of this book in which an authoritative and exhaustive categorization of doctrines, principles, and applications is presented. However, no definitive list exists that correctly identifies and classifies all gospel doctrines and principles. And frankly, such a list would be of little value. Rather, the purpose of the framework is for *you* to explore, to experiment, and to exercise faith in the Lord as *you learn for yourself* "the doctrine of the kingdom" (Doctrine and Covenants 88:77) and come to "know of the true points of [the Savior's] doctrine" (3 Nephi 21:6) by asking questions and searching for answers.

Some doctrines, such as the nature of the Godhead and the Atonement, clearly are doctrines that answer the question of "why." And some principles, such as faith in Jesus Christ and repentance, are principles that directly answer the question of "what." But some gospel topics seemingly could be categorized appropriately as either doctrines or principles. For example, is obedience a doctrine or a principle? Is scripture study a principle or an application? These are precisely the kinds of searching questions the framework is intended to help us identify and explore.

If one uses the plan of happiness as a doctrinal starting point, then obedience can be interpreted as a principle linked to the plan (see Figure 3).

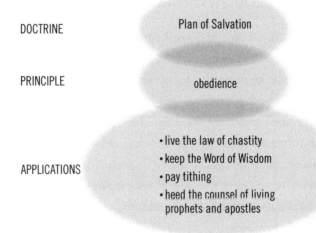

DOCTRINE   Plan of Salvation

PRINCIPLE   obedience

APPLICATIONS
- live the law of chastity
- keep the Word of Wisdom
- pay tithing
- heed the counsel of living prophets and apostles

Figure 3

However, if obedience is used as the starting point, then a different series of questions must be addressed and different answers are obtained (see Figure 4).

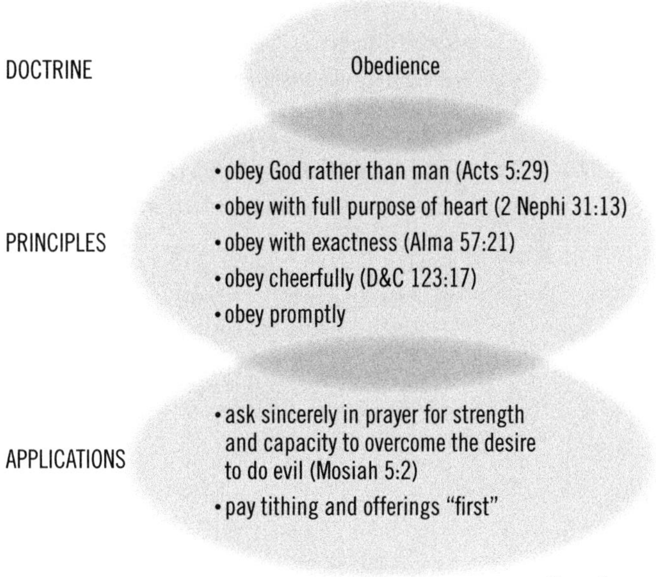

DOCTRINE   Obedience

PRINCIPLES
- obey God rather than man (Acts 5:29)
- obey with full purpose of heart (2 Nephi 31:13)
- obey with exactness (Alma 57:21)
- obey cheerfully (D&C 123:17)
- obey promptly

APPLICATIONS
- ask sincerely in prayer for strength and capacity to overcome the desire to do evil (Mosiah 5:2)
- pay tithing and offerings "first"

Figure 4

If one uses the principle of "treasure up in your minds continually the words of life" (Doctrine and Covenants 84:85) as a starting point, then using the method of researching specific topics in daily scripture study may be viewed as an application (see Figure 5).

However, if scripture study is used as a principle and as the starting point, then a different series of questions must be addressed, and different answers are obtained (see Figure 6).

Please do not become frustrated by the fact that what appears to be a doctrine in one example may legitimately be considered to be a principle in another illustration—or a principle as an application. Doctrines, principles, and applications are not discrete, separate, and unrelated truths that can easily be arranged in a chart or

PRINCIPLE   Treasure Up . . . the Words of Life

- read and study the standard works by topic
- read the standard works and search for patterns
  and themes
- read and study the monthly messages from the
APPLICATIONS   First Presidency in the *Ensign* and *Liahona*
- read and study the messages presented in
  general conference
- read and study the latest messages from
  the latter-day prophets and apostles at
  ChurchofJesusChrist.org

Figure 5

PRINCIPLE   Scripture Study

- read regularly
- ask in sincere prayer for understanding
- invite the help of the Holy Ghost
- work diligently
APPLICATIONS   - ponder
- record thoughts, feelings, and impressions
- use a question or concern as a context or
  framework for reading, studying, and pondering

Figure 6

a spreadsheet. Rather, they are often overlapping and interrelated truths, as shown in Figure 7.

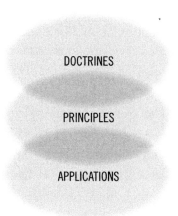

Figure 7

Remember that the primary purpose of the framework is to help a learner employ the pattern of asking, seeking, and knocking. Do not be too concerned or worried about quickly finding the right answer. Rather, focus upon asking the right questions. If the questions are right, then we are much more likely to obtain inspired and insightful answers as we work, ponder, search, and pray.

In What Ways Does the Framework Help Me to Learn?

At this point in the chapter, you likely are asking yourself a valid and important question. In what ways does this framework help a person learn and live gospel truths? Some perspective about the distinctive dispensation in which we are living can help to answer this vital question.

The greatest and last of all gospel dispensations was introduced through the Prophet Joseph Smith. It was necessary in this final dispensation "that a whole and complete and perfect union, and welding together of dispensations, and keys, and powers, and glories should take place, and be revealed from the days of Adam even to the present time. And not only this, but those things which never have been revealed from the foundation of the world, but have been kept hid from the wise and prudent, shall be revealed . . . in this, the dispensation of the fulness of times" (Doctrine and Covenants 128:18). The Prophet Joseph explained, "All the ordinances and duties that ever have been required by the Priesthood, under the directions and commandments of the Almighty in any of the dispensations, shall all be had in the last dispensation, . . . bringing to pass the restoration spoken of by the mouth of all the Holy Prophets" (*Teachings: Joseph Smith,* 511).

Joseph further proclaimed that preparatory to the Second Coming of the Lord Jesus Christ, "the dispensation of the fullness of times will bring to light the things that have been revealed in all former dispensations; also other things that have not been before revealed" (*Teachings: Joseph Smith,* 510–11). As the Apostle Paul declared, "In the dispensation of the fulness of times [God will] gather together in one all things in Christ, both which are in heaven, and which are on earth; even in him" (Ephesians 1:10).

See video segment 18

Thus, the overarching purpose of this concluding dispensation is to gather together in one all things in Christ. Let me suggest that the principle of *gather together in one* applies in a practical way to our daily learning and living of the gospel.

Some members of the Church seem to compartmentalize the restored gospel into a lengthy list of things to do—as separate and unrelated "applications" to be accomplished and checked off. Daily scripture study—check. Personal and family prayer—check. Tithing—check. Family home evening—check. Temple attendance—check. Home and visiting teaching—check. But the purification, the joy, the happiness, the continuing conversion, and the spiritual power and protection that come from "yielding [our] hearts unto God" (Helaman 3:35) cannot be obtained merely by performing and checking off all of the gospel things we are supposed to do. Consistently completing the various tasks without experiencing the mighty change of heart and becoming more devoted disciples will not produce the spiritual strength we need to withstand the evils and opposition of the latter days. Rather, the power of the Savior's gospel to bless and guide us comes from the connectedness and interrelatedness of its doctrines, principles, and practices. Only as we *gather together in one* all things in Christ can we diligently strive to become what God desires us to become (see Matthew 5:48; 3 Nephi 12:48). And the framework of doctrines, principles, and applications is a tool that can help us investigate and learn about the interrelatedness of gospel truths and practices.

As we learn and link the revealed truths from all dispensations, we receive eyes that can see and ears that can hear (see Doctrine and Covenants 136:32). The gospel is not a routine checklist comprised of discrete tasks; it is a magnificent tapestry of truth "fitly framed" (Ephesians 2:21) and woven together.

The principle of *gather together in one* can aid us in changing the conventional checklist into a unified, integrated, and complete whole and in receiving the transforming power of the gospel of Jesus Christ in our daily lives. Let me provide several examples of what I am suggesting.

In our homes and classes, we frequently learn about the great plan of happiness, the infinite Atonement, moral agency, individual accountability, and sacred covenants. Typically, however, these vital doctrines and principles are considered separately rather than in relation to each other. As we *gather together in one* these eternal truths, we see and hear more clearly our relationship to the Father and the Son, our divine potential and destiny as sons and daughters of God, the nature of eternal progression, and the simplicity, order, and beauty of the Father's plan (see Alma 42:4–9, 14–23).

In our homes and classes we frequently discuss and learn about sacrifice, obedience, and consecration. Typically, however, these important principles are considered separately rather than in relation to each other. As we *gather together in one* these related truths, we see more clearly the pathway of discipleship and hear the admonitions to come unto the Savior, to bridle all of our passions (see Alma 38:12), "to perform every word of command with exactness" (Alma 57:21), to strip ourselves of pride (see Alma 5:28), and to "offer [our] whole souls as an offering unto him" (Omni 1:26).

In our homes and classes we frequently emphasize the importance of regular scripture study, personal and family prayer, and Church attendance. Typically, however, these important practices are considered separately rather than in relation to each other. As we *gather together in one* these complementary habits of holiness, we hear more clearly the priesthood injunction to "receive the Holy Ghost." We recognize these sincere practices as essential in inviting the Spirit of the Lord into our lives. Studying, praying, and worshipping are not isolated and independent items on a checklist of things to do. Rather, each of these righteous practices is an important element in an overarching spiritual quest to fulfill the mandate to receive and retain the Holy Ghost. Fundamentally, all gospel teachings and activities are centered on coming unto the Savior and having the power of the Holy Ghost in our lives.

In the Church we have quorums, auxiliaries, effective programs, and inspiring meetings. Typically, however, organizations and functions are considered separately rather than in relation to each other. As we *gather together in one* all of the program purposes and reasons for gathering, we see and hear more clearly the role of these vital activities in knitting our hearts "together in unity and in love" (Mosiah 18:21) and in caring for the temporal and spiritual needs of our brothers and sisters. Programs and meetings are not events to be managed; rather, they are opportunities to minister to individuals and families.

Priesthood authority, priesthood keys, and eternal truths have been restored to the earth in the dispensation of the fulness of times. The fulness of the Savior's gospel and the work of His Church have been reestablished and are rolling forth throughout the world. Today you and I have vital roles to play in enlarging the borders of Zion (see Doctrine and Covenants 82:14). In this final dispensation we are responsible to *gather together in one* eternal truths about the Father's plan and the Savior's Atonement, about ordinances, covenants, discipleship, and the constant companionship of the Holy Ghost, and about knitting our hearts together in unity and in love by fulfilling our divine duty to serve and rescue the one.

The framework of doctrines, principles, and applications can assist us in asking, seeking, and knocking in such a way that we more effectively gather together all things in one, in Christ—in this the dispensation of the fulness of times.

IMPORTANT QUESTIONS TO PONDER

Consider the following question—and answer it honestly and candidly. Please do not quickly give the obviously appropriate answer or the response you think you should give. Take a few moments to reflect on "things as they really are" (Jacob 4:13) before answering.

"In your living of the gospel of Jesus Christ and in your serving and teaching both at home and in the Church, have you focused primarily on doctrines, on principles, or on applications?"

I have asked this question of tens of thousands of members of the Church, including priesthood and auxiliary leaders all over the world. The consistency of their answers is stunning. My posing of the question typically engenders a few moments of awkward silence. And then heads begin to nod and with knowing smiles come the responses, nearly always: "applications." It is interesting to me how reluctant members usually are to acknowledge the actual answer to this question—even though the answer almost always is recognized immediately.

Now please ponder some additional questions.

"Why? Why do many members tend typically to focus on applications more than on doctrines and principles?"

Here is a sample of some of the answers I have received to this follow-up question.

"Focusing upon applications is easier."

"Applications are more tangible."

"I can control applications."

"I can accomplish things quicker by focusing on applications."

"My professional experience has taught me to get things done and make things happen—so I gravitate to applications."

"I am not comfortable teaching doctrine."

"I do not know the doctrine well enough to teach it with confidence."

*See video
segment 5*

Somehow we seem to be drawn to applications as the primary way to "fix" things, to make life better, to be "doers of the word," to achieve desired outcomes, and to help the Church operate effectively. And far too often we emphasize applications without the necessary understanding and divorced from the doctrinal context.

We may focus on applications because we like to believe and

feel like we are in control, because we have confidence in our own experience and expertise—"the arm of flesh" (2 Nephi 4:34)—or because we are only doing what we have seen other teachers and leaders do. We may think as we serve in a quorum or auxiliary, "I am going to make this happen; I am going to manage this the right way." We all would do well to remember that The Church of Jesus Christ of Latter-day Saints is the Lord's Church, and He is able to do His own work (see 2 Nephi 27:20).

I find it both noteworthy and troubling that in the dispensation of the fulness of times, a season in the history of the world during which all things are to be gathered together in one in Christ, many members are exasperatingly engaged in creating ever longer lists of detailed and disconnected gospel applications.

Whatever the reasons, emphasizing applications to the exclusion of fundamental doctrines and principles does not produce spiritual power, protection, and direction. To be clear, I am not suggesting that doctrines and principles are wholly and routinely ignored; rather, I am suggesting that applications, such as some of those presented earlier in this chapter as items on the lengthy "to do" lists of many members, tend to receive disproportionate and excessive attention. I also am not suggesting that applications should never be studied, learned, or taught. Appropriate applications are necessary but can never stand alone. What is needed is a balance among doctrines, principles, and applications. And for many conscientious and diligent members, a serious imbalance exists.

Consider the basic responsibility of Melchizedek Priesthood holders to serve as home teachers. What do you think would happen if each man in a congregation of 100 elders and high priests were invited to write down on a three-by-five card the doctrinal reasons for home teaching? Would the answers be similar or

See video segment 17

different? Would the same scriptural references be used to support those answers? Or would the answers vary dramatically? My experience suggests that many men can describe *how* to home teach; far fewer can explain *why* we home teach.

Men in the Church who do not perform their priesthood duty as home teachers are not lazy; they simply have not understood the relevant doctrine and principles. Such men undoubtedly have been both taught and told. They may *know* that a home teacher is to watch over, be with, and strengthen (see Doctrine and Covenants 20:53)—but they have not learned, they do not *understand,* and they are not *intelligent* (as the word *intelligence* is used in the scriptures).

If a man *understands*—both in his mind and in his heart, by the power of the Holy Ghost—the doctrines of the plan of happiness and of the priesthood, then he will be a faithful home teacher. Always! The reasons, the purposes, the answers are found in the doctrine. An understanding of true doctrines and correct principles will improve behavior more effectively than the study of behavior will improve behavior. The answers always are found in the doctrines and principles of the restored gospel of Jesus Christ.

Let me recommend one additional question that can be helpful in a wide range of situations and circumstances. Given that true doctrine, understood, changes attitudes and behavior, and assuming you are a priesthood leader who is concerned about effective home teaching, you might ask yourself the following question:

What doctrines and principles, if *understood,* would change the attitudes and behaviors of brethren who are not fulfilling their duty as home teachers?

Consider how this simple question can be used as a starting point for almost any issue or concern. And imagine what could happen if husbands and wives, parents and children, priesthood and auxiliary leaders, and members of the Church humbly invited the guidance of the Holy Ghost, forthrightly counseled together, and diligently worked to answer questions (such as the examples that follow) by asking, seeking, and knocking.

- What doctrines and principles, if *understood,* would change the attitudes and behaviors of a man or woman who is struggling with or addicted to pornography?
- What doctrines and principles, if *understood,* would help me to strengthen my marriage?
- What doctrines and principles, if *understood,* would change the attitudes and behaviors of endowed members who are not presently worthy to worship in the temple?
- What doctrines and principles, if *understood,* would help me prepare for marriage and family responsibilities?
- What doctrines and principles, if *understood,* would protect our children from worldly pressures to violate the law of chastity?
- What doctrines and principles, if *understood,* would change the attitudes and behaviors of members who are hesitant to open their mouths and share the gospel?
- What doctrines and principles, if *understood,* would change the attitudes and behaviors of members who are not regularly studying the scriptures?

The answers always are in the doctrine and principles!

"And now, as *the preaching of the word* had a great tendency to lead the people to do that which was just—yea, it had had more powerful effect upon the minds of the people than the sword, or anything else, which had happened unto them—therefore Alma thought it was expedient that they should try *the virtue of the word of God*" (Alma 31:5; emphasis added).

See video segment 16

Note that it was the virtue of the word of God and the preaching of the word, or the doctrines and principles of the gospel—not simply clever applications—that led the people to do that which was just. There is no spiritual power or enduring impact from even the most innovative and impressive applications if they are divorced from the fundamental doctrines and principles of the restored gospel. Conversely, applications built upon, arising from, and connected with a firm foundation of fundamental doctrines and principles provide great spiritual power.

As Ammon explained, "Behold, how many thousands of our brethren has he loosed from the pains of hell; and they are brought to sing redeeming love, and this because of *the power of his word which is in us,* therefore have we not great reason to rejoice?" (Alma 26:13; emphasis added).

The answers always are in the doctrines and principles! And the doctrines and principles need to be in us!

SUMMARY

As Nephi concluded his explanation of why Christ was baptized, of the importance of following the Savior into the waters of baptism and receiving the Holy Ghost, of enduring to the end, and of repentance and baptism as the gate to the strait and narrow path, he declared:

"And now, behold, my beloved brethren, this is the way; and there is none other way nor name given under heaven whereby man can be saved in the kingdom of God. And now, behold, *this is the doctrine of Christ,* and the only and true doctrine of the Father, and of the Son, and of the Holy Ghost, which is one God, without end. Amen" (2 Nephi 31:21; emphasis added).

We are blessed to live in a day when the gospel of Jesus Christ has been restored to the earth, even the dispensation of the fulness of times. Available to us are eternal truths and guidelines, priesthood authority and keys, sacred scriptures, and living prophets, all of which will enable and fortify us to "withstand the evil day, having done all, that ye may be able to stand" (Doctrine and Covenants 27:15). And with great blessings come great responsibilities. "For of him unto whom much is given much is required" (Doctrine and Covenants 82:3). Thus, each and every member of The Church of Jesus Christ of Latter-day Saints bears a *personal* responsibility to learn and live the truths of the Savior's restored gospel and to receive by proper authority the ordinances of salvation. We should not expect the Church as an organization to teach or tell us all of the things we need to know and do to become devoted disciples and endure valiantly to the end (see Doctrine and Covenants 121:29). Rather, our individual responsibility is to learn what we should learn, to live as we know we should live, and to become what the Master would have us become.

See video segment 19

And the answers always are in the doctrines and principles!

QUESTIONS TO CONSIDER

1. What can and should I do in my learning and serving to achieve a better balance among doctrines, principles, and applications?
2. What can and should I do in my learning and studying to "gather together in one all things in Christ"?
3. What doctrines and principles, if understood, would help me press forward in becoming what the Master would have me become?

YOUR OWN QUESTIONS TO CONSIDER

1. _____

2. _____

3. _____

The video segments related to this chapter can be found at
desbook.com/learning

RELATED READINGS
FOR CHAPTER FOUR

The answers that satisfy the deepest questions of the soul, the understanding that enables us to learn from life's most challenging experiences, and the perspective that helps us to see "things as they really are" always are found in the doctrines and principles of the restored gospel of Jesus Christ. However, simply knowing *about* the doctrines of salvation is not sufficient. Rather, each of us should strive to become like Ammon and his missionary companions and have "the power of his word . . . *in* us" (Alma 26:13; emphasis added).

"And now, as the preaching of the *word* had a great tendency to lead the people to do that which was just—yea, it had had more powerful effect upon the minds of the people than the sword, or anything else, which had happened unto them—therefore Alma thought it was expedient that they should try *the virtue of the word of God*" (Alma 31:5; emphasis added).

The framework of doctrines, principles, and applications is a useful tool as we strive to receive "the power of his word in us" and "try the virtue of the word of God." The following readings focus upon the foundational doctrines and principles related to marriage, the work of proclaiming the gospel, and the role of a physical body in the plan of salvation.

Marriage Is Essential to His Eternal Plan

From *Ensign,* June 2006, 82–87

The Doctrinal Ideal of Marriage

We have been counseled strongly by the First Presidency to devote our best efforts to the strengthening of marriage and the home. Such instruction has never been more needed in the world than it is today, as the sanctity of marriage is attacked and the importance of the home is undermined.

Even though the Church and its programs support marriage and family and generally are successful at doing so, we should always remember this basic truth: no instrumentality or organization can take the place of the home or perform its essential functions (see First Presidency letter, February 11, 1999; or "Policies, Announcements, and Appointments," 80). I direct my message to you primarily as men and women, as husbands and wives, and as mothers and fathers and secondarily as priesthood and auxiliary leaders in the Church. I desire to discuss the essential role of eternal marriage in our Heavenly Father's plan of happiness.

We will focus on the doctrinal ideal of marriage. My hope is that a review of our eternal possibilities and a reminder about who we are and why we are here in mortality will provide direction, comfort, and sustaining hope for us all, regardless of our marital status or personal present circumstances. The disparity between the doctrinal ideal of marriage and the reality of daily life may seem at times to be quite large, but you gradually are doing and becoming much better than you probably recognize.

I invite you to keep in mind the following questions as we discuss principles related to eternal marriage.

Question 1: In my own life, am I striving to become a better husband or a wife, or preparing to be a husband or a wife, by understanding and applying these basic principles?

Question 2: As a priesthood or auxiliary leader, am I helping those I serve to understand and apply these basic principles, thereby strengthening marriage and the home?

As we prayerfully ponder these questions and consider our own marriage relationships and our responsibilities in the Church, I testify the Spirit of the Lord will enlighten our minds and teach us the things we need to do and to improve (see John 14:26).

Why Marriage Is Essential

In "The Family: A Proclamation to the World," the First Presidency and Council of the Twelve Apostles proclaim "that marriage between a man and a woman is ordained of God and that the family is central to the Creator's plan for the eternal destiny of His children" ("The Family: A Proclamation to the World," 102). This keynote sentence of the proclamation teaches us much about the doctrinal significance of marriage and emphasizes the primacy of marriage and family in the Father's plan. Righteous marriage is a commandment and an essential step in the process of creating a loving family relationship that can be perpetuated beyond the grave.

Two compelling doctrinal reasons help us to understand why eternal marriage is essential to the Father's plan.

Reason 1: The natures of male and female spirits complete and perfect each other, and therefore men and women are intended to progress together toward exaltation.

The eternal nature and importance of marriage can be fully understood only within the overarching context of the Father's plan for His children. "All human beings—male and female—are created in the image of God. Each is a beloved spirit son or daughter of heavenly parents, and . . . has a divine nature and destiny" ("The Family: A Proclamation," 102). The great plan of happiness enables the spirit sons and daughters of Heavenly Father to obtain physical bodies, to gain earthly experience, and to progress toward perfection.

"Gender is an essential characteristic of individual premortal, mortal, and eternal identity and purpose" ("The Family: A Proclamation," 102) and in large measure defines who we are, why we are here upon the earth, and what we are to do and become. For divine purposes, male and female spirits are different, distinctive, and complementary.

After the earth was created, Adam was placed in the Garden of Eden. Importantly, however, God said it was "not good that the man should be alone" (Genesis 2:18; Moses 3:18), and Eve became Adam's companion and helpmeet. The unique combination of spiritual, physical, mental, and emotional capacities of both males and females was needed to implement the plan of happiness. Alone, neither the man nor the woman could fulfill the purposes of his or her creation.

By divine design, men and women are intended to progress together toward perfection and a fulness of glory. Because of their distinctive temperaments and capacities, males and females each bring to a marriage relationship unique perspectives and experiences. The man and the woman contribute differently but equally to a oneness and a unity that can be achieved in no other way. The man completes and perfects the woman and the woman completes and perfects the man as they learn from and mutually strengthen and bless each other. "Neither is the man without the woman, neither the woman without the man, *in the Lord*" (1 Corinthians 11:11; emphasis added).

Reason 2: By divine design, both a man and a woman are needed to bring children into mortality and to provide the best setting for the rearing and nurturing of children.

The commandment given anciently to Adam and Eve to multiply and replenish the earth remains in force today. "God has commanded that the sacred powers of procreation are to be employed only between man and woman, lawfully wedded as husband and wife. . . . The means by which mortal life is created [are] divinely appointed" ("The Family: A Proclamation," 102). Thus, marriage between a man and a woman is the authorized channel through which premortal spirits enter mortality. Complete sexual abstinence before marriage and total fidelity within marriage protect the sanctity of this sacred channel.

A home with a loving and loyal husband and wife is the supreme setting in which children can be reared in love and righteousness and in which the spiritual and physical needs of children can be met. Just as the unique characteristics of both males and females contribute to the completeness of a marriage relationship, so those same characteristics are vital to the rearing, nurturing, and teaching of children. "Children are entitled to birth within the bonds of matrimony, and to be reared by a father and a mother who honor marital vows with complete fidelity" ("The Family: A Proclamation," 102).

Guiding Principles

The two doctrinal reasons we have reviewed about the importance of eternal marriage in the Father's plan of happiness suggest guiding principles for those who are preparing to marry, for those who are married, and for our service in the Church.

Principle 1: The importance of eternal marriage can be understood only within the context of the Father's plan of happiness.

We frequently speak about and highlight marriage as a fundamental unit of society, as the foundation of a strong nation, and as a vital sociological and cultural institution. But the restored gospel helps us to understand that it is so much more!

Do we perhaps talk about marriage without adequately teaching the importance of marriage in the Father's plan? Emphasizing marriage without linking it to the simple and fundamental doctrine of the plan of happiness cannot provide sufficient direction, protection, or hope in a world that grows increasingly confused and wicked. We would all do well to remember the teaching of Alma—that "God gave unto [the children of men] commandments, *after* having made known unto them the plan of redemption" (Alma 12:32; emphasis added).

Elder Parley P. Pratt expressed beautifully the blessings that come to us as we learn about, understand, and strive to apply in our lives the doctrinal ideal of marriage:

"It was Joseph Smith who taught me how to prize the endearing relationships of father and mother, husband and wife; of brother and sister, son and daughter.

"It was from him that I learned that the wife of my bosom might be secured to me for time and all eternity; and that the refined sympathies and affections which endeared us to each other emanated from the fountain of divine eternal love. . . .

"I had loved before, but I knew not why. But now I loved—with a pureness—an intensity of elevated, exalted feeling, which would lift my soul from the transitory things of this grovelling sphere and expand it as the ocean. . . . In short, I could now love with the spirit and with the understanding also.

"Yet, at that time, my dearly beloved brother, Joseph Smith, had . . . merely lifted a corner of the veil and given me a single glance into eternity" (*Autobiography of Parley P. Pratt,* 297–98).

As men and women, as husbands and wives, and as Church leaders, can we see how the importance of eternal marriage can be understood only within the context of the Father's plan of happiness? The doctrine of the plan leads men and women to hope and prepare for eternal marriage, and it defeats the fears and overcomes the uncertainties that may cause some individuals to delay or avoid marriage. A correct understanding of the plan also strengthens our resolve to steadfastly honor the covenant of eternal marriage. Our individual learning, our teaching, and our testifying in both the home and at church will be magnified as we ponder and more fully understand this truth.

Principle 2: Satan desires that all men and women might be miserable like unto himself.

Lucifer relentlessly assails and distorts the doctrines that matter most to us individually, to our families, and to the world. Where is the adversary focusing his most direct and diabolical attacks? Satan works unremittingly to confuse understanding about gender, to promote the premature and unrighteous use of procreative power, and to hinder righteous marriage precisely because marriage is ordained of God and the family is central to the plan of happiness. The adversary's attacks upon eternal marriage will continue to increase in intensity, frequency, and sophistication.

Because today we are engaged in a war for the welfare of

marriage and the home, in my latest reading of the Book of Mormon I paid particular attention to the ways the Nephites prepared for their battles against the Lamanites. I noted that the people of Nephi "were *aware of the intent* of [their enemy], and therefore they did prepare to meet them" (Alma 2:12; emphasis added). As I read and studied, I learned that *understanding the intent of an enemy* is a key prerequisite to effective preparation. We likewise should consider the intent of our enemy in this latter-day war.

The Father's plan is designed to provide direction for His children, to help them become happy, and to bring them safely home to Him. Lucifer's attacks on the plan are intended to make the sons and daughters of God confused and unhappy and to halt their eternal progression. The overarching intent of the father of lies is that all of us would become "miserable like unto himself" (2 Nephi 2:27), and he works to warp the elements of the Father's plan he hates the most. Satan does not have a body, he cannot marry, and he will not have a family. And he persistently strives to confuse the divinely appointed purposes of gender, marriage, and family. Throughout the world, we see growing evidence of the effectiveness of Satan's efforts.

More recently the devil has attempted to combine and legally validate confusion about gender and marriage. As we look beyond mortality and into eternity, it is easy to discern that the counterfeit alternatives the adversary advocates can never lead to the completeness that is made possible through the sealing together of a man and a woman, to the happiness of righteous marriage, to the joy of posterity, or to the blessing of eternal progression.

Given what we know about our enemy's intent, each of us should be especially vigilant in seeking personal inspiration as to how we can protect and safeguard our own marriages—and how we can learn and teach correct principles in the home and in our Church assignments about the eternal significance of gender and of the role of marriage in the Father's plan.

Principle 3: The ultimate blessings of love and happiness are obtained through the covenant relationship of eternal marriage.

The Lord Jesus Christ is the focal point in a covenant marriage relationship. Imagine a triangle with the Savior positioned at the apex, a woman at the base of one corner, and a man at the base of the other corner. Now consider what happens in the relationship between the man and the woman as they individually and steadily "come unto Christ" and strive to be "perfected in Him" (Moroni 10:32). Because of and through the Redeemer, the man and the woman come closer together.

As a husband and wife are each drawn to the Lord (see 3 Nephi 27:14), as they learn to serve and cherish one another, as they share life experiences and grow together and become one, and as they are blessed through the uniting of their distinctive natures, they begin to realize the fulfillment that our Heavenly Father desires for His children. Ultimate happiness, which is the very object of the Father's plan, is received through the making and honoring of eternal marriage covenants.

As men and women, as husbands and wives, and as Church leaders, one of our paramount responsibilities is to help young men and women learn about and prepare for righteous marriage through our personal example. As young women and men observe worthiness, loyalty, sacrifice, and the honoring of covenants in our marriages, then those youth will seek to emulate the same principles in their courting and marriage relationships. As young people notice that we have made the comfort and convenience of our eternal companion our highest priority, then they will become less self-centered and more able to give, to serve, and to create an equal and enduring companionship. As young women and men perceive mutual respect, affection, trust, and love between a husband and a wife, then they will strive to cultivate the same characteristics in their lives. Our children and the youth of the Church will learn the most from what we do and what we are—even if they remember relatively little of what we say.

Unfortunately many young members of the Church today are fearful of and stumble in their progress toward eternal marriage because they have seen too much of divorce in the world and of broken covenants in their homes and in the Church.

Eternal marriage is not merely a temporary legal contract that can be terminated at any time for almost any reason. Rather, it is a sacred covenant with God that can be binding in time and throughout all eternity. Faithfulness and fidelity in marriage must not simply be attractive words spoken in sermons; rather, they should be principles evident in our own covenant marriage relationships.

As we consider the importance of our personal example, do you and I discern areas where we need to improve? Is the Holy Ghost inspiring our minds and softening our hearts and encouraging us to do and to become better? As priesthood and auxiliary leaders, are we focusing our efforts on strengthening marriage and the home?

Husbands and wives need time together to fortify themselves and their homes against the attacks of the adversary. As we strive to magnify our callings in the Church, are we unintentionally hindering husbands and wives and mothers and fathers from fulfilling their sacred responsibilities in the home? For example, do we sometimes schedule unnecessary meetings and activities in a way that interferes with the essential relationship between a husband and a wife and their relationships with children?

As we sincerely ponder these questions, I am confident the Spirit is even now helping and will continue to help each of us learn the things we should do at home and in the Church.

The Spiritual Resources We Need

Our responsibilities to learn and understand the doctrine of the plan, to uphold and be examples of righteous marriage, and to teach correct principles in the home and at church may cause us to wonder if we are equal to the task. We are ordinary people who must accomplish a most extraordinary work.

Many years ago, Sister Bednar and I were busy trying to meet the countless competing demands of a young and energetic family—and of Church, career, and community responsibilities. One evening after the children were asleep, we talked at length about how effectively we were attending to all of our important priorities. We realized that we would not receive the promised blessings in eternity if we did not honor more fully the covenant we had made in mortality. We resolved together to do and to be better as a husband and a wife. That lesson learned so many years ago has made a tremendous difference in our marriage.

The sweet and simple doctrine of the plan of happiness provides precious eternal perspective and helps us understand the importance of eternal marriage. We have been blessed with all of the spiritual resources we need. We have the fulness of the doctrine of Jesus Christ. We have the Holy Ghost and revelation. We have saving ordinances, covenants, and temples. We have priesthood and prophets. We have the holy scriptures and the power of the word of God. And we have The Church of Jesus Christ of Latter-day Saints.

I testify that we have been blessed with all of the spiritual resources we need to learn about, to teach, to strengthen, and to defend righteous marriage—and that indeed we can live together in happiness as husbands and wives and families in eternity.

Becoming a Missionary

From *Ensign,* November 2005, 44–47

All of us who have received the holy priesthood bear the sacred obligation to bless the nations and families of the earth by proclaiming the gospel and inviting all to receive by proper authority the ordinances of salvation. Many of us have served as full-time missionaries, some of us presently are serving as full-time missionaries, and all of us now are serving and will continue to serve as lifelong missionaries. We are missionaries every day in our families, in our schools, in our places of employment, and in our communities. Regardless of our age, experience, or station in life, we are all missionaries.

Proclaiming the gospel is not an activity in which we periodically and temporarily engage. And our labors as missionaries certainly are not confined to the short period of time devoted to full-time missionary service in our youth or in our mature years. Rather, the obligation to proclaim the restored gospel of Jesus Christ is inherent in the oath and covenant of the priesthood into which we enter. Missionary work essentially is a priesthood responsibility, and all of us who hold the priesthood are the Lord's authorized servants on the earth and are missionaries at all times and in all places—and we always will be. Our very identity as holders of the priesthood and the seed of Abraham is in large measure defined by the responsibility to proclaim the gospel.

A Frequently Asked Question

In meetings with young members of the Church around the world, I often invite those in attendance to ask questions. One of the questions I am asked most frequently by young men is this: "What can I do to prepare most effectively to serve as a full-time missionary?" Such a sincere question deserves a serious response.

My dear young brethren, the single most important thing you can do to prepare for a call to serve is to *become* a missionary long before you go on a mission. Please notice that in my answer I emphasized *becoming* rather than *going.* Let me explain what I mean.

In our customary Church vocabulary, we often speak of *going* to church, *going* to the temple, and *going* on a mission. Let me be so bold as to suggest that our rather routine emphasis on *going* misses the mark.

The issue is not going to church; rather, the issue is worshipping and renewing covenants as we attend church. The issue is not going to or through the temple; rather, the issue is having in our hearts the spirit, the covenants, and the ordinances of the Lord's house. The issue is not going on a mission; rather, the issue is becoming a missionary and serving throughout our entire life with all of our heart, might, mind, and strength. It is possible for a young man to *go* on a mission and not *become* a missionary, and this is not what the Lord requires or what the Church needs.

My earnest hope for each of you young men is that you will not simply go on a mission—but that you will become missionaries long before you submit your mission papers, long before you receive a call to serve, long before you are set apart by your stake president, and long before you enter the MTC.

The Principle of Becoming

Elder Dallin H. Oaks has taught us most effectively about the challenge to become something instead of just doing expected things or performing certain actions:

"The Apostle Paul taught that the Lord's teachings and teachers were given that we may all attain 'the measure of the stature of the fulness of Christ' (Ephesians 4:13). This process requires far more than acquiring knowledge. It is not even enough for us to be *convinced* of the gospel; we must act and think so that we are *converted* by it. In contrast to the institutions of the world, which teach us to *know* something, the gospel of Jesus Christ challenges us to *become* something. . . .

" . . . It is not enough for anyone just to go through the motions. The commandments, ordinances, and covenants of the gospel are not a list of deposits required to be made in some heavenly account. The gospel of Jesus Christ is a plan that shows us how to become what our Heavenly Father desires us to become" ("The Challenge to Become," 32).

The challenge to become applies precisely and perfectly to missionary preparation. Obviously, the process of becoming a missionary does not require a young man to wear a white shirt and tie to school every day or to follow the missionary guidelines for going to bed and getting up, although most parents certainly would support that idea. But you can increase in your desire to serve God (see Doctrine and Covenants 4:3), and you can begin to think as missionaries think, to read what missionaries read, to pray as missionaries pray, and to feel what missionaries feel. You can avoid the worldly influences that cause the Holy Ghost to withdraw, and you can grow in confidence in recognizing and responding to spiritual promptings. Line upon line and precept upon precept, here a little and there a little, you can gradually become the missionary you hope to be and the missionary the Savior expects.

You will not suddenly or magically be transformed into a prepared and obedient missionary on the day you walk through the front door of the Missionary Training Center. What you have become in the days and months and years prior to your missionary service is what you will be in the MTC. In fact, the nature of the transition through which you will pass in the MTC will be a strong indicator of your progress in becoming a missionary.

As you enter the MTC, you obviously will miss your family, and many aspects of your daily schedule will be new and challenging. But for a young man well on his way to becoming a missionary, the basic adjustment to the rigors of missionary work and lifestyle will not be overwhelming, burdensome, or constraining. Thus, a key element of raising the bar includes working to become a missionary before going on a mission.

Fathers, do you understand your role in helping your son to become a missionary before he goes on a mission? You and your wife are key in the process of his becoming a missionary. Priesthood and auxiliary leaders, do you recognize your responsibility to assist parents and to help every young man become a missionary before he goes on a mission? The bar also has been raised for parents and for all members of the Church. Prayerful pondering of the principle of becoming will invite inspiration tailored to the specific needs of your son or to the young men whom you serve.

The preparation I am describing is not oriented only toward your missionary service as a nineteen- or twenty- or twenty-one-year-old young man. Brethren, you are preparing for a lifetime of missionary work. As holders of the priesthood, we are missionaries always. If you truly progress in the process of becoming a missionary, both before going on a mission and in the mission field, then when the day arrives for your honorable release as a full-time missionary, you will depart from your field of labor and return to your family—but you will never cease your missionary service. A priesthood holder is a missionary at all times and in all places. A missionary is who and what we are as bearers of the priesthood and as the seed of Abraham.

The Seed of Abraham

The heirs of all the promises and covenants made by God to Abraham are referred to as *the seed of Abraham* (see Bible Dictionary, "Seed of Abraham," 771). These blessings are obtained only by obedience to the laws and ordinances of the gospel of Jesus Christ. The process of becoming a missionary is directly related to understanding who we are as the seed of Abraham.

Abraham was a great prophet who desired righteousness and was obedient to all of the commandments he received from God, including the command to offer as a sacrifice his precious son, Isaac. Because of his steadfastness and obedience, Abraham is often referred to as the father of the faithful, and Heavenly Father established a covenant with and promised great blessings to Abraham and his posterity:

"Because thou hast done this thing, and hast not withheld thy son, thine only son:

"That in blessing I will bless thee, and in multiplying I will multiply thy seed as the stars of the heaven, and as the sand which is upon the sea shore; and thy seed shall possess the gate of his enemies;

"And in thy seed shall all the nations of the earth be blessed; because thou has obeyed my voice" (Genesis 22:16–18).

Thus, Abraham was promised a great posterity and that the nations of the earth would be blessed through that posterity.

How are the nations of the earth blessed through the seed of Abraham? The answer to this important question is found in the book of Abraham:

"And I will make of thee [Abraham] a great nation, and I will bless thee above measure, and make thy name great among all nations, and thou shalt be a blessing unto thy seed after thee, that in their hands they shall bear this ministry and Priesthood unto all nations;

"And I will bless them through thy name; for as many as receive this Gospel shall be called after thy name, and shall be accounted thy seed, and shall rise up and bless thee, as their father" (Abraham 2:9–10).

We learn in these verses that Abraham's faithful heirs would have the blessings of the gospel of Jesus Christ and the authority of the priesthood. Thus, the phrase "bear this ministry and Priesthood unto all nations" refers to the responsibility to proclaim the gospel of Jesus Christ and to invite all to receive by proper priesthood authority the ordinances of salvation. Truly, great responsibility rests upon the seed of Abraham in these latter days.

How do these promises and blessings relate to us today? Either by literal lineage or adoption, every Latter-day Saint is a rightful heir to the promises made by God to Abraham. We are the seed of Abraham. One of the primary reasons we receive a patriarchal blessing is to help us more fully understand who we are as the posterity of Abraham and to recognize the responsibility that rests upon us.

You and I, today and always, are to bless all peoples in all the nations of the earth. You and I, today and always, are to bear witness of Jesus Christ and declare the message of the Restoration.

You and I, today and always, are to invite all to receive the ordinances of salvation. Proclaiming the gospel is not a part-time priesthood obligation. It is not simply an activity in which we engage for a limited time or an assignment we must complete as members of The Church of Jesus Christ of Latter-day Saints. Rather, missionary work is a manifestation of our spiritual identity and heritage. We were foreordained in the premortal existence and born into mortality to fulfill the covenant and promise God made to Abraham. We are here upon the earth at this time to magnify the priesthood and to preach the gospel. That is who we are, and that is why we are here—today and always.

You may enjoy music, athletics, or be mechanically inclined, and someday you may work in a trade or a profession or in the arts. As important as such activities and occupations can be, they do not define who we are. First and foremost, we are spiritual beings. We are children of God and the seed of Abraham:

"For whoso is faithful unto the obtaining these two priesthoods of which I have spoken, and the magnifying their calling, are sanctified by the Spirit unto the renewing of their bodies.

"They become the sons of Moses and of Aaron and the seed of Abraham, and the church and kingdom, and the elect of God" (Doctrine and Covenants 84:33–34).

We have been given much, and much is required of us. May you young men more fully understand who you are as the seed of Abraham and become missionaries long before you go on a mission. After coming back to your homes and families, may you returned missionaries always be missionaries. And may all of us rise up as servants of God and bless the nations of the earth with greater testimony and spiritual power than we ever have before.

THINGS AS THEY REALLY ARE

From *Ensign,* June 2010, 16–25

I long have been impressed with the simple and clear definition of truth set forth in the Book of Mormon: "The Spirit speaketh the truth and lieth not. Wherefore, it speaketh of things as they really are, and of things as they really will be; wherefore, these things are manifested unto us plainly, for the salvation of our souls" (Jacob 4:13; see also Doctrine and Covenants 93:24).

We will focus upon the first major element of truth identified in this verse: "things as they really are." We first will review several key elements of our Heavenly Father's plan of happiness as the doctrinal foundation for knowing and understanding things as they really are. We then will consider methods of attack used by the adversary to distract us from or inhibit our capacity to discern things as they really are. And finally, we will discuss the responsibilities that rest upon the rising generation. You will need to be obedient, to honor sacred covenants, and to discern things consistently as they really are in today's world that grows ever more confused and wicked.

Our Divine Destiny

In "The Family: A Proclamation to the World," the First Presidency and Council of the Twelve Apostles declare that as spirit sons and daughters of God, we "accepted His plan by which His children could obtain a physical body and gain earthly experience to progress toward perfection and ultimately realize [our] divine destiny as heirs of eternal life" ("The Family: A Proclamation," 102). Please note the primary importance of obtaining a physical body in the process of progressing toward our divine destiny.

The Prophet Joseph Smith taught with clarity the importance of our physical bodies:

"We came to this earth that we might have a body and present it pure before God in the celestial kingdom. The great principle of happiness consists in having a body. The devil has no body, and herein is his punishment. He is pleased when he can obtain the tabernacle of man, and when cast out by the Savior he asked to go into the herd of swine, showing that he would prefer a swine's body to having none. All beings who have bodies have power over those who have not. . . .

"The devil has no power over us only as we permit him; the moment we revolt at anything which comes from God, the devil takes power" (*Teachings: Joseph Smith,* 211, 214).

Our physical bodies make possible a breadth, a depth, and an intensity of experience that simply could not be obtained in our premortal estate. President Boyd K. Packer, President of the Quorum of the Twelve Apostles, has taught, "Our spirit and our body are combined in such a way that our body becomes an instrument of our mind and the foundation of our character" ("The Instrument of Your Mind," 2). Thus, our relationships with other people, our capacity to recognize and act in accordance with truth, and our ability to obey the principles and ordinances of the gospel of Jesus Christ are amplified through our physical bodies. In the classroom of mortality, we experience tenderness, love, kindness, happiness, sorrow, disappointment, pain, and even the challenges of physical limitations in ways that prepare us for eternity. Simply stated, there are lessons we must learn and experiences we must have, as the scriptures describe, "according to the flesh" (1 Nephi 19:6; Alma 7:12–13).

Apostles and prophets consistently have taught the mortal and eternal importance of our bodies. Paul declared:

"Know ye not that ye are the temple of God, and that the Spirit of God dwelleth in you?

"If any man defile the temple of God, him shall God destroy; for the temple of God is holy, which temple ye are" (1 Corinthians 3:16–17).

And in this dispensation the Lord revealed that "the spirit and the body are the soul of man" (Doctrine and Covenants 88:15). A truth that really is and always will be is that the body and the spirit constitute our reality and identity. When body and spirit are inseparably connected, we can receive a fulness of joy; when they are separated, we cannot receive a fulness of joy (see Doctrine and Covenants 93:33–34).

The Father's plan is designed to provide direction for His children, to help them become happy, and to bring them safely home to Him with resurrected, exalted bodies. Lucifer labors to make the sons and daughters of God confused and unhappy and to hinder their eternal progression. The overarching intent of the father of lies is that all of us become "miserable like unto himself" (2 Nephi 2:27), and he works to distort the elements of the Father's plan he hates the most.

Satan does not have a body, and his eternal progress has been halted. Just as water flowing in a riverbed is stopped by a dam, so the adversary's eternal progress is thwarted because he does not have a physical body. Because of his rebellion, Lucifer has denied himself all of the mortal blessings and experiences made possible through a tabernacle of flesh and bones. He cannot learn the lessons that only an embodied spirit can learn. He cannot marry or enjoy the blessings of procreation and family life. He cannot abide the reality of a literal and universal resurrection of all mankind. One of the potent scriptural meanings of the word *damned* is illustrated in his inability to continue developing and becoming like our Heavenly Father.

Because a physical body is so central to the Father's plan of happiness and our spiritual development, we should not be surprised that Lucifer seeks to frustrate our progression by tempting us to use our bodies improperly. One of the ultimate ironies of eternity is that the adversary, who is miserable precisely because he has no physical body, invites and entices us to share in his misery through the improper use of our bodies. The very tool he does not have and cannot use is thus the primary target of his attempts to lure us to physical and spiritual destruction.

The Adversary's Attacks

The adversary attempts to influence us both to misuse our physical bodies and to minimize the importance of our bodies. These two methods of attack are important for us to recognize and to repel.

When any of Heavenly Father's children misuse their physical tabernacles by violating the law of chastity, by using drugs and addictive substances, by disfiguring or defacing themselves, or by worshipping the false idol of body image, whether their own or that of others, Satan is delighted. To those of us who know and understand the plan of salvation, any defiling of the body is rebellion and a denial of our true identity as sons and daughters of God (see Mosiah 2:36–37; Doctrine and Covenants 64:34–35).

I cannot tell you all the ways whereby you may misuse your bodies, "for there are divers ways and means, even so many that I cannot number them" (Mosiah 4:29). You know what is right and what is wrong, and you have the individual responsibility to learn for yourself "by study and also by faith" (Doctrine and Covenants 88:118) the things you should and should not do and the doctrinal reasons you should and should not do those things. I testify that as you desire to so learn, as you "watch yourselves, and your thoughts, and your words, and your deeds, and observe the commandments of God, and continue in the faith of what ye have heard concerning the coming of our Lord, even unto the end of your lives" (Mosiah 4:30), you will be spiritually enlightened and protected. And according to your faithfulness and diligence, you will have the power to discern the deception and repel the attacks of the adversary as he tempts you to misuse your physical body.

Satan also strives to entice the sons and daughters of God to minimize the importance of their physical bodies. This particular type of attack is most subtle and diabolical. I want to provide several examples of how the adversary can pacify and lull us away into a sense of carnal security (see 2 Nephi 28:21) and encourage us to put at risk the earthly learning experiences that caused us to shout for joy in the premortal existence (see Job 38:7).

For example, all of us can find enjoyment in a wide range of wholesome, entertaining, and engaging activities. But we diminish the importance of our bodies and jeopardize our physical well-being by going to unusual and dangerous extremes searching for an ever-greater and more exhilarating adrenaline "rush." We may rationalize that surely nothing is wrong with such seemingly innocent exploits and adventures. However, putting at risk the very instrument God has given us to receive the learning experiences of mortality—merely to pursue a thrill or some supposed fun, to bolster ego, or to gain acceptance—truly minimizes the importance of our physical bodies.

Sadly, some young men and young women in the Church today ignore "things as they really are" and neglect eternal relationships for digital distractions, diversions, and detours that have no lasting value. My heart aches when a young couple—sealed together in the house of the Lord for time and for all eternity by the power of the holy priesthood—experiences marital difficulties because of the addicting effect of excessive video gaming or online socializing. A young man or woman may waste countless hours, postpone or forfeit vocational or academic achievement, and ultimately sacrifice cherished human relationships because of mind- and spirit-numbing video and online games. As the Lord declared, "Wherefore, I give unto them a commandment . . . : Thou shalt not idle away thy time, neither shalt thou bury thy talent that it may not be known" (Doctrine and Covenants 60:13).

You may now be asking yourself, "But, Brother Bednar, you began by talking about the importance of a physical body in our eternal progression. Are you suggesting that video gaming and various types of computer-mediated communication can play a role in minimizing the importance of our physical bodies?" That is precisely what I am declaring. Let me explain.

We live at a time when technology can be used to replicate reality, to augment reality, and to create virtual reality. For example, a medical doctor can use software simulation to gain valuable experience performing a complicated surgical operation without ever putting a human patient at risk. A pilot in a flight simulator repeatedly can practice emergency landing procedures that could save many lives. And architects and engineers can use innovative technologies to model sophisticated design and construction methods that decrease the loss of human life and damage to buildings caused by earthquakes and other natural disasters.

In each of these examples, a high degree of fidelity in the

simulation or model contributes to the effectiveness of the experience. The term *fidelity* denotes the similarity between reality and a representation of reality. Such a simulation can be constructive if the fidelity is high and the purposes are good—for example, providing experience that saves lives or improves the quality of life.

However, a simulation or model can lead to spiritual impairment and danger if the fidelity is high and the purposes are bad—such as experimenting with actions contrary to God's commandments or enticing us to think or do things we would not otherwise think or do "because it is only a game."

I raise an apostolic voice of warning about the potentially stifling, suffocating, suppressing, and constraining impact of some kinds of cyberspace interactions and experiences upon our souls. The concerns I raise are not new; they apply equally to other types of media, such as television, movies, and music. But in a cyber world, these challenges are more pervasive and intense. I plead with you to beware of the sense-dulling and spiritually destructive influence of cyberspace technologies that are used to produce high fidelity and that promote degrading and evil purposes.

If the adversary cannot entice us to misuse our physical bodies, then one of his most potent tactics is to beguile you and me as embodied spirits to disconnect gradually and physically from things as they really are. In essence, he encourages us to think and act as if we were in our premortal, unembodied state. And, if we let him, he can cunningly employ some aspects of modern technology to accomplish his purposes. Please be careful of becoming so immersed and engrossed in pixels, texting, earbuds, twittering, online social networking, and potentially addictive uses of media and the Internet that you fail to recognize the importance of your physical body and miss the richness of person-to-person communication. Beware of digital displays and data in many forms of computer-mediated interaction that can displace the full range of physical capacity and experience.

Read carefully the following quote describing an intense romantic relationship a woman had with a cyberspace boyfriend. And note how the medium of communication minimized the importance of the physical body: "And so PFSlider [the man's screen name] became my everyday life. All the tangible stuff fell away. My body did not exist. I had no skin, no hair, no bones. All desire had converted itself into a cerebral current that reached nothing but my frontal lobe. There was no outdoors, no social life, no weather. There was only the computer screen and the phone, my chair, and maybe a glass of water" (Meghan Daum, "Virtual Love," *The New Yorker,* Aug. 25 and Sept. 1, 1997, 82).

In contrast, we need to heed the admonition of Paul: "That every one of you should know how to possess his vessel in sanctification and honour" (1 Thessalonians 4:4).

Consider again the example I mentioned earlier of a young couple recently married in the house of the Lord. An immature or misguided spouse may devote an inordinate amount of time to playing video games, chatting online, or in other ways allowing the digital to dominate things as they really are. Initially the investment of time may seem relatively harmless, rationalized as a few minutes of needed relief from the demands of a hectic daily schedule. But important opportunities are missed for developing and improving interpersonal skills, for laughing and crying together, and for creating a rich and enduring bond of emotional intimacy. Progressively, seemingly innocent entertainment can become a form of pernicious enslavement.

To feel the warmth of a tender hug from an eternal companion or to see the sincerity in the eyes of another person as testimony is shared—all of these things experienced as they really are through the instrument of our physical body—could be sacrificed for a high-fidelity fantasy that has no lasting value. If you and I are not vigilant, we can become "past feeling" (1 Nephi 17:45), as did Laman and Lemuel long ago.

Let me provide another example of disconnecting gradually and physically from things as they really are. Today a person can enter into a virtual world, such as Second Life, and assume a new identity. An individual can create an avatar, or a cyberspace persona, that conforms to his or her own appearance and behavior. Or a person can concoct a counterfeit identity that does not correlate in any way to things as they really are. However closely the assumed new identity approximates the individual, such behavior is the essence of things as they really are not. Earlier I defined the fidelity of a simulation or model. I now emphasize the importance of personal fidelity—the correspondence between an actual person and an assumed, cyberspace identity. Please note the lack of personal fidelity in the following episode as reported in the *Wall Street Journal*:

Ric Hoogestraat is "a burly [53-year-old] man with a long gray ponytail, thick sideburns and a salt-and-pepper handlebar mustache. . . . [Ric spends] six hours a night and often 14 hours at a stretch on weekends as Dutch Hoorenbeek, his six-foot-nine, muscular . . . cyber-self. The character looks like a younger, physically enhanced version of [Ric]. . . .

" . . . [He] sits at his computer with the blinds drawn. . . . While his wife, Sue, watches television in the living room, Mr. Hoogestraat chats online with what appears on the screen to be a tall, slim redhead.

"He's never met the woman outside of the computer world of Second Life, a well-chronicled digital fantasyland. . . . He's never so much as spoken to her on the telephone. But their relationship has taken on curiously real dimensions. They own two dogs, pay a mortgage together and spend hours [in their cyberspace world] shopping at the mall and taking long motorcycle rides. . . . Their bond is so strong that three months ago, Mr. Hoogestraat asked Janet Spielman, the 38-year-old Canadian woman who controls the redhead, to become his virtual wife.

"The woman he's legally wed to is not amused. 'It's really devastating,' says Sue Hoogestraat, . . . who has been married to Mr. Hoogestraat for seven months" (Alexandra Alter, "Is This Man Cheating on His Wife?" *Wall Street Journal,* Aug. 10, 2007, W8, W1).

Please understand. I am not suggesting all technology is inherently bad; it is not. Nor am I saying we should not use its **many** capabilities in appropriate ways to learn, to communicate, to lift and brighten lives, and to build and strengthen the Church; of course we should. But I am raising a warning voice that we should not squander and damage authentic relationships by obsessing over contrived ones. "Nearly 40% of men and 53% of women who play online games said their virtual friends were equal to or better than their real-life friends, according to a survey of 30,000 gamers conducted by . . . a recent Ph.D. graduate from Stanford University. More than a quarter of gamers [who responded indicated that] the emotional highlight of the past week occurred in a computer world." (Alter, "Is This Man Cheating?" W8.)

How important, how enduring, and how timely is the Lord's definition of truth: "things as they really are." The prophet Alma asked, "O then, is not this real?" (Alma 32:35). He was speaking of light and good so discernible they can be tasted. Indeed, "they who dwell in [the Father's] presence . . . see as they are seen, and know as they are known, having received of his fulness and of his grace" (Doctrine and Covenants 76:94).

My beloved brothers and sisters, beware! To the extent personal fidelity decreases in computer-mediated communications and the purposes of such communications are distorted, perverted, and wicked, the potential for spiritual disaster is dangerously high. I implore you to turn away immediately and permanently from such places and activities (see 2 Timothy 3:5).

Now I would like to address an additional characteristic of the adversary's attacks. Satan often offers an alluring illusion of anonymity. Lucifer always has sought to accomplish his work in secret (see Moses 5:30). Remember, however, that apostasy is not anonymous simply because it occurs in a blog or through a fabricated identity in a chat room or virtual world. Immoral thoughts, words, and deeds always are immoral, even in cyberspace. Deceitful acts supposedly veiled in secrecy, such as illegally downloading music from the Internet or copying CDs or DVDs for distribution to friends and families, are nonetheless deceitful. We are all accountable to God, and ultimately we will be judged of Him according to our deeds and the desires of our hearts (see Alma 41:3). "For as [a man] thinketh in his heart, so is he" (Proverbs 23:7).

The Lord knows who we really are, what we really think, what we really do, and who we really are becoming. He has warned us that "the rebellious shall be pierced with much sorrow; for their iniquities shall be spoken upon the housetops, and their secret acts shall be revealed" (Doctrine and Covenants 1:3).

I have raised a voice of warning about only a few of the spiritual hazards in our technologically oriented and rapidly changing world. Let me say again: neither technology nor rapid change in or of itself is good or evil; the real challenge is to understand both within the context of the eternal plan of happiness. Lucifer will encourage you to misuse and to minimize the importance of your physical body. He will attempt to substitute the monotony of virtual repetition for the infinite variety of God's creations and convince us we are merely mortal things to be acted upon instead of eternal souls blessed with moral agency to act for ourselves. Deviously, he entices embodied spirits to forfeit the blessings and learning experiences "according to the flesh" (1 Nephi 19:6; Alma 7:12–13) that are made possible through the Father's plan of happiness and the Atonement of His Only Begotten Son.

For your happiness and protection, I invite you to study more diligently the doctrine of the plan of salvation—and to prayerfully ponder the truths we have reviewed. I offer two questions for consideration in your personal pondering and prayerful studying:

1. Does the use of various technologies and media invite or impede the constant companionship of the Holy Ghost in your life?

2. Does the time you spend using various technologies and media enlarge or restrict your capacity to live, to love, and to serve in meaningful ways?

You will receive answers, inspiration, and instruction from the Holy Ghost suited to your individual circumstances and needs. I repeat and affirm the teaching of the Prophet Joseph: "All beings who have bodies have power over those who have not. The devil has no power over us only as we permit him."

These eternal truths about the importance of our physical bodies will fortify you against the deception and the attacks of the adversary. One of my deepest desires for you is an ever-increasing testimony of and appreciation for the Resurrection—even your own resurrection with a celestial, exalted body "because of your faith in [the Lord Jesus Christ] according to the promise" (Moroni 7:41).

The Rising Generation

In October of 1997, Elder Neal A. Maxwell (1926–2004) of the Quorum of the Twelve Apostles visited Brigham Young

University–Idaho to speak in a devotional. During the day he was on the campus, we talked together about a variety of gospel topics in general and about the youth of the Church in particular. I remember Elder Maxwell making a statement that greatly impressed me. He said, "The youth of this generation have a greater capacity for obedience than any previous generation."

He then indicated that his statement was based upon a truth taught by President George Q. Cannon (1827–1901), First Counselor in the First Presidency: "God has reserved spirits for this dispensation who have the courage and determination to face the world, and all the powers of the evil one, visible and invisible, to proclaim the gospel and maintain the truth and establish and build up the Zion of our God fearless of all consequences. He has sent these spirits in this generation to lay the foundation of Zion never more to be overthrown, and to raise up a seed that will be righteous, and that will honor God, and honor Him supremely, and be obedient to Him under all circumstances" (in *Journal of Discourses,* 11:230).

Parents and Church leaders frequently emphasize that the young men and young women of this generation have been reserved for this season in the history of the world and are some of the most valiant of Heavenly Father's children. Indeed, such statements are true. But I often have wondered if young people hear this description so often that it becomes overused and trite—and that its importance and deep implications may be overlooked. We know that "unto whom much is given much is required" (Doctrine and Covenants 82:3). And the teachings of President Cannon and Elder Maxwell help us to understand more fully what is required of us today. You and I are to be valiant and "obedient to Him under all circumstances." Thus, obedience is the principal weapon upon which the rising generation must rely in the latter-day battle between good and evil.

We rejoice that the Lord through His authorized servants has "raised the bar" for the young men and young women of today. Given what we know about who we are and why we are here upon the earth, such inspired direction is welcomed and appreciated. And we should recognize that Lucifer incessantly strives to "lower the bar" by coaxing us to misuse and minimize the importance of our physical bodies.

The Savior has warned us repeatedly to beware of deception by the adversary:

"Jesus answered, and said unto them: Take heed that no man deceive you; . . .

"For in those days there shall also arise false Christs, and false prophets, and shall show great signs and wonders, insomuch, that, if possible, they shall deceive the very elect, who are the elect according to the covenant . . .

"And whoso treasureth up my word, shall not be deceived" (Joseph Smith—Matthew 1:5, 22, 37).

Obedience opens the door to the constant companionship of the Holy Ghost. And the spiritual gifts and abilities activated by the power of the Holy Ghost enable us to avoid deception—and to see, to feel, to know, to understand, and to remember things as they really are. You and I have been endowed with a greater capacity for obedience precisely for these reasons. Moroni declared:

"Hearken unto the words of the Lord, and ask the Father in the name of Jesus for what things soever ye shall stand in need. Doubt not, but be believing, and begin as in times of old, and come unto the Lord with all your heart, and work out your own salvation with fear and trembling before him.

"Be wise in the days of your probation; strip yourselves of all uncleanness; ask not, that ye may consume it on your lusts, but ask with a firmness unshaken, that ye will yield to no temptation, but that ye will serve the true and living God" (Mormon 9:27–28).

As we heed that inspired counsel, we can and will be blessed to recognize and repel the attacks of the adversary—today and in the days that lie ahead. We can and will fulfill our foreordained responsibilities and contribute to the work of the Lord in all the world.

I testify that God lives and is our Heavenly Father. He is the author of the plan of salvation. Jesus is the Christ, the Redeemer, whose body was bruised, broken, and torn for us as He offered the atoning sacrifice. He is resurrected, He lives, and He stands at the head of His Church in these latter days. To be "encircled about eternally in the arms of his love" (2 Nephi 1:15) will be a real and not a virtual experience.

I testify we can and will be blessed with the courage and determination to face the world and all the powers of the evil one. Righteousness will prevail. No unhallowed hand can stop this work from progressing. These are things as they really are and as they really will be.

SOURCES CITED

Ashton, Marvin J. "'There Are Many Gifts.'" *Ensign,* November 1987, 20–22.

Briggs, E. C. "Brother Joseph Smith." *Saints' Herald* 31, no. 25 (21 June 1884):396–97.

Cannon, George Q. *Gospel Truth: Discourses and Writings of George Q. Cannon,* comp. Jerreld L. Newquist. Salt Lake City: Deseret Book, 1987.

———. *Life of Joseph Smith the Prophet.* Salt Lake City: Deseret Book, 1986.

"The Family: A Proclamation to the World." *Ensign,* November 1995, 102.

Hafen, Bruce C. "'Eve Heard All These Things and Was Glad.'" In *Women in the Covenant of Grace,* ed. Dawn Hall Fletcher and Susette Fletcher Green. Salt Lake City: Deseret Book, 1994, 16–33.

Hinckley, Gordon B. "With All Thy Getting Get Understanding." *Ensign,* August 1988, 2–5.

———. *Teachings of Gordon B. Hinckley.* Salt Lake City: Deseret Book, 1997.

Hymns of The Church of Jesus Christ of Latter-day Saints. Salt Lake City: The Church of Jesus Christ of Latter-day Saints, 1985.

Journal of Discourses. 26 vols. London: Latter-day Saints' Book Depot, 1854–56.

Lectures on Faith. Salt Lake City: Deseret Book, 1985.

Lee, Harold B. *Ye Are the Light of the World.* Salt Lake City: Deseret Book, 1974.

———. "When Your Heart Tells You Things Your Mind Does Not Know." *New Era,* February 1971, 2–4.

McKay, David O. "True Education." *Improvement Era,* March 1957, 141–42.

Morris, Michael R. "A Fire Burning within Me." *Liahona,* October 2011, 66–67.

———. "'One Talk' in Papua New Guinea." *Ensign,* February 1995, 22–29.

Nelson, Russell M. "The Gathering of Scattered Israel." *Ensign,* November 2006, 79–82.

———. "A Testimony of the Book of Mormon." *Ensign,* November 1999, 69–72.

Oaks, Dallin H. "The Aaronic Priesthood and the Sacrament." *Ensign,* November 1998, 37–40.

———. "The Challenge to Become." *Ensign,* November 2000, 32–34.

Packer, Boyd K. "The Instrument of Your Mind and the Foundation of Your Character." *Brigham Young University 2002–2003 Speeches.* Provo, UT: Brigham Young University, 2003.

———. "Little Children." *Ensign,* November 1986, 16–18.

———. "Scriptures," *Ensign,* November 1982, 51–53.

"Policies, Announcements, and Appointments." *Ensign,* June 1999, 80.

Pratt, Parley P. *Autobiography of Parley P. Pratt,* ed. Parley P. Pratt Jr. Salt Lake City: Deseret Book, 1938.

Romney, Marion G. *Learning for the Eternities,* comp. George J. Romney. Salt Lake City: Deseret Book, 1977.

Smith, Joseph. *History of The Church of Jesus Christ of Latter-day Saints.* 7 vols. Salt Lake City: The Church of Jesus Christ of Latter-day Saints, 1932–1951.

———. "History of the Life of Joseph Smith." Manuscript, Archives of The Church of Jesus Christ of Latter-day Saints, 1832.

Smith, Joseph III. "Last Testimony of Sister Emma." *Saints' Herald* 26, no. 19 (1 October 1879):289–90.

Teachings of Presidents of the Church: Brigham Young. Salt Lake City: The Church of Jesus Christ of Latter-day Saints, 1997.

Teachings of Presidents of the Church: Joseph Smith. Salt Lake City: The Church of Jesus Christ of Latter-day Saints, 2007.

Young, Brigham. *Discourses of Brigham Young,* sel. John A. Widtsoe. Salt Lake City: Deseret Book, 1946.

INDEX

About the Author

Elder David A. Bednar was ordained a member of the Quorum of the Twelve Apostles in 2004. Prior to his call, he had served as an Area Seventy, regional representative, and stake president. He served a mission to southern Germany, then attended Brigham Young University, where he received a bachelor's degree and a master's degree. He received a PhD in organizational behavior from Purdue University and was a professor of business management at Texas Tech University and the University of Arkansas. Elder Bednar served as the president of BYU–Idaho from 1997 to 2004. He and his wife, Susan, are the parents of three sons.